GHOSTS OF BELL COUNTY TEXAS

GHOSTS OF BELL COUNTY TEXAS

CHET SOUTHWORTH

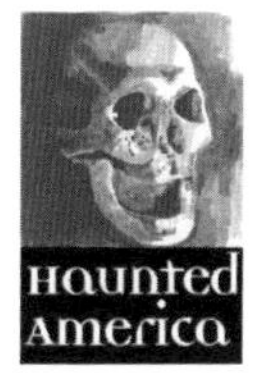

Published by Haunted America
A Division of The History Press
Charleston, SC
www.historypress.com

Front cover: Original City of Killeen water well. *Author photo.*
Back cover: Maxdale Bridge. *Author photo*; inset: Downtown Killeen circa 1890. *Courtesy of the Killeen City Library System and used with permission of the City of Killeen.*

First published 2018

Manufactured in the United States

ISBN 9781467139779

Library of Congress Control Number: 2018942438

Many thanks to the
Killeen Area Paranormal Society,
the Killeen City Library System,
Light Paranormal Investigations of Temple, Texas,
and especially my wife, Barbara.

Without their help, this book could not have been completed.

The photographs on the cover and on pages 12, 13, 16, 19, 26, 45, 55, 62 and 69 are courtesy of the Killeen City Library System and used with permission of the City of Killeen.

CONTENTS

PREFACE

There have been many stories told of a variety of inexplicable events that have occurred in and around Bell County, Texas, over the decades. Evidence of human habitation has been found in excavations showing the region was inhabited for tens of thousands of years before Robertson's Colony was established in the 1830s. Indian unrest was common, and the settlers relied on Little River Fort to protect them. Death was a common occurrence in early Bell County, as both Indian raids and the hostile environment took their toll. By 1850, the population of Bell County stood around 660. Bell County was officially formed in 1850 and named for Peter H. Bell. The county seat was established in the area now known as Belton, and it remains so today.[1]

The largest city in Bell County and the most active hot spot for paranormal activity is the city of Killeen. Named after railroad assistant general manager Frank P. Killeen, the city was instantly turned into the agricultural, financial and social hub for western Bell County, Texas, and was a popular place to visit.

Death was not uncommon in the Wild West, and Bell County was no different. With several saloons and banks, the old towns of Killeen, Temple, Belton and Salado attracted their fair share of all types of people to fill the dirt-covered streets. No doubt some of them were fine, upstanding citizens. Some of them were of less savory character. Some of them may still be wandering around the county, searching for an end of their journey, a final resting spot.

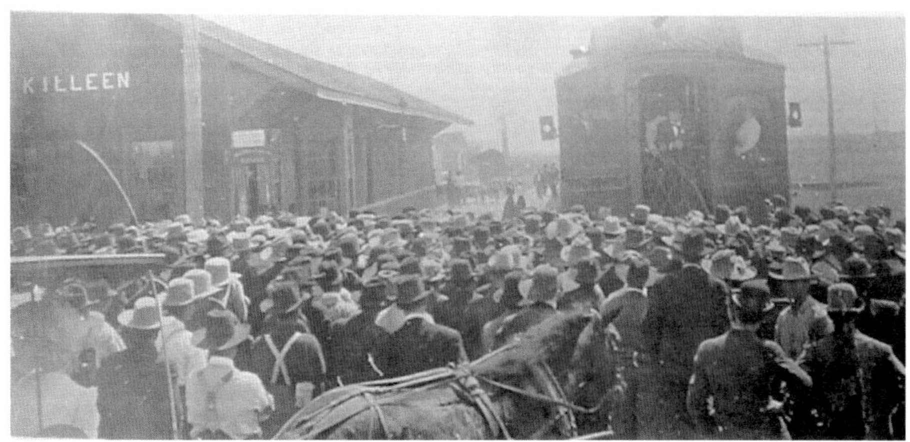

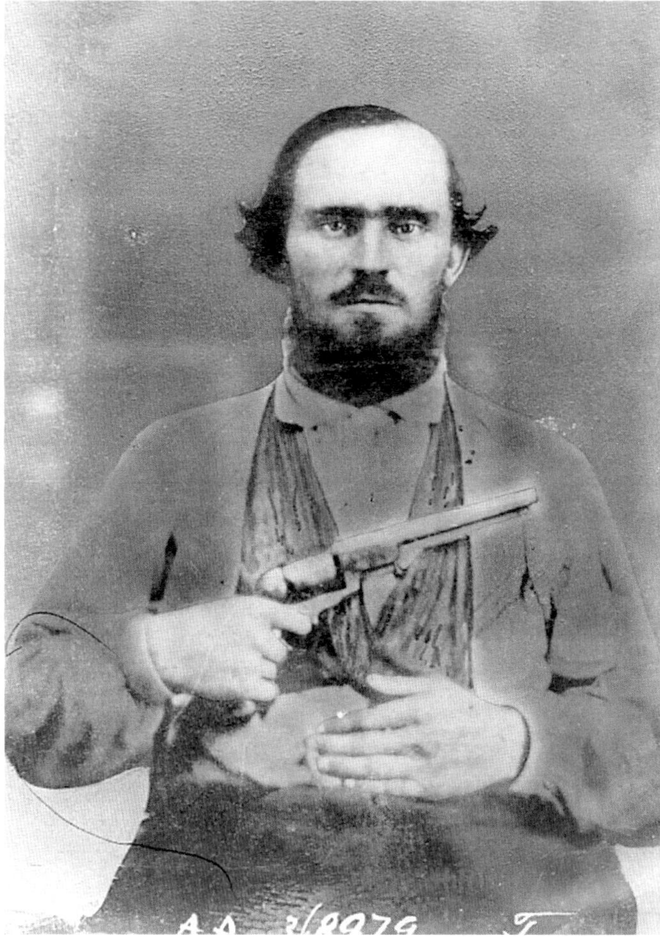

Above: William Jennings Bryan political rally at the Killeen train station, 1909.

Left: Joe H. Boydstun.

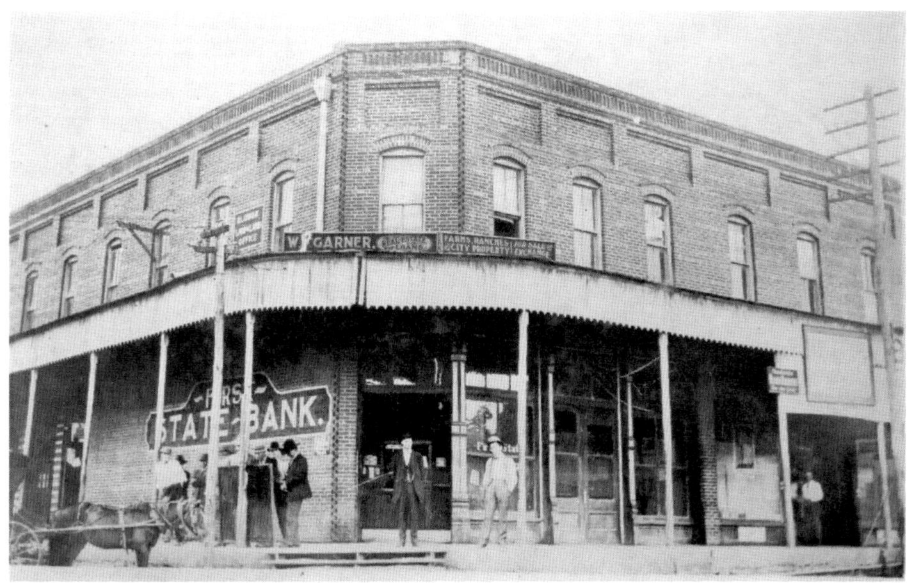

First State Bank on the corner of Avenue D and Gray, circa 1910.

While Killeen continues to be regarded as a legendary habitat for haunts, the rest of Bell County does not lag far behind. To truly understand the spirits that continue to roam the area, it is necessary to study the makeup of ghosts, the types of entities that may exist and the possible manifestations they are reported to have in the material world we live in. Then and only then will it be possible to review the variety of paranormal entities that have been reported to wander around in and about Bell County.

1
Stage Ghost

Stillhouse Hollow

Back in the mid-1860s came the end of the War Between the States. After valiantly fighting for Southern independence, many former soldiers returned home to find their property in ruins, their homes repossessed or, worse, confiscated by Yankees as payback for their service in the Confederate army.

The men tried to find work, but hard currency was sparse and jobs scarce. Most of the young men were unskilled, having been in the military most of their lives. Some, with no other work available, returned to the one skill they had been trained in, the way of the gun.

Bob was one of them. Bob was reported to have served in the cavalry and was familiar with ambushes as well as hit-and-run tactics. With no home left and desperate for funds to buy a ranch, Bob turned to earning his living with a gun by robbing stagecoaches as they traveled north from Austin. No one knew his real name or would admit to it if they did. He earned the name Bob by what he did when he worked his trade.

Stages used to run infrequently in southern Bell County, but there was a stage station just north of the Lampasas River. The route to the station required stages to cross the river. As there was no bridge back then, the stage crossed through shallows close to where the Maxdale Bridge now stands. Climbing the far bank slowed stagecoaches and provided Bob a perfect opportunity to relieve them and their northern passengers of valuables.

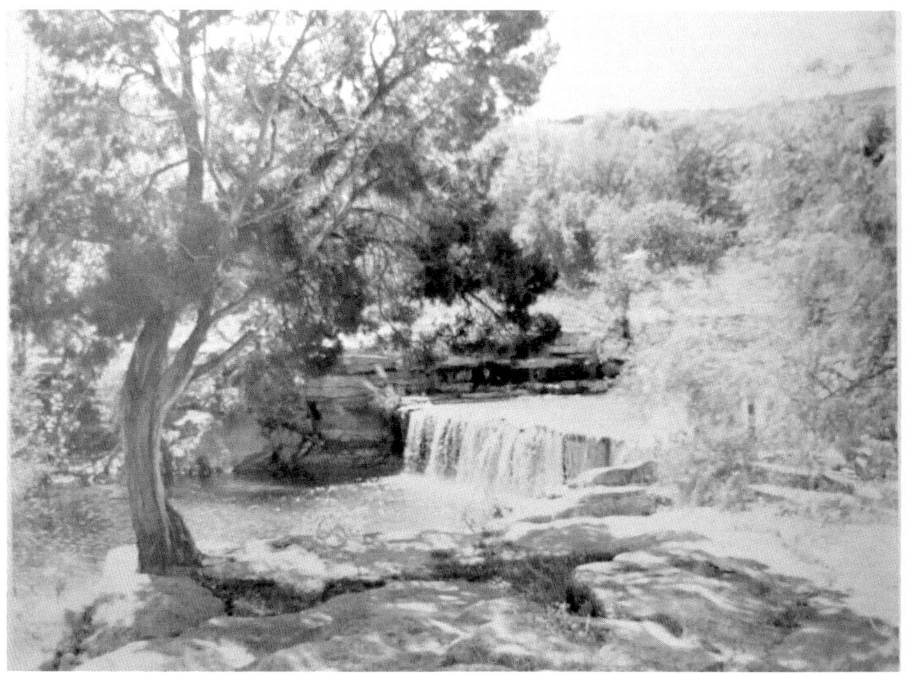

Stillhouse Hollow.

While it is true that Bob held up stagecoaches, his manner of doing so was quite unusual. Halting the stage when it slowed, and with his face covered by a kerchief to hide his identity, he would have the passengers disembark, ask them where they were from and only take things from northerners. To those who claimed to be from Texas, he would bob his head politely and allow them to return to the coach without taking anything. Thus, the name Bob arose when people spoke of him.

Bob secreted his ill-gotten gains in a small cave in the side of Stillhouse Hollow, through which the Lampasas River ran. He slowly built up his stake for his new life. He wanted to settle down and hang up his guns for good. He had amassed quite a bit of gold, silver and northern currency and was ready to quit when fate intervened to prevent this happy ending.

During his final holdup, a northerner pulled a gun and there was a shootout. A woman was killed, and her ghost has been reportedly seen hanging around the area, especially the area of the old stage station on the north side of the river just east of the highway.

Bob was mortally injured but managed to ride away from the scene. He made it almost to the side of the large hollow before falling from his horse.

Weak and still bleeding, he pulled himself along toward his hideout, his treasure trove, but he was too injured. He died on the edge of Stillhouse Hollow, within a few hundred feet of his lair.

His body and the treasure he amassed were never found. His spirit was rumored to be anchored there, slowly drifting between his body and his loot.

Not knowing the history of the hollow and the Lampasas River that ran through it, the U.S. Army Corps of Engineers built a dam and flooded the area, creating a lake and burying the cave forever. Soft moaning has been heard at the edge of the lake, the cries of a spirit unable to pass through the water to visit the treasure Bob loved so much. Some claim the moaning is just the wind passing through the trees, but the locals know the truth. Woe betide any humans who seem to come to seek Bob's treasure or even come too close to it.

One couple decided to camp out on the side of Stillhouse Hollow Lake. Since the Stillhouse Hollow Lake recreational area prohibits camping, they decided to camp in the wilderness next to the lake. They didn't bother to ask permission from the owners of the property. No doubt they would have warned them of the danger and advised them to leave.

That evening, the couple heard the moaning in the distance, seemingly coming closer, but laughed it off as just the wind. Later that night, they heard something rustling in the bushes near their camp. The husband bravely took a flashlight and went to investigate. We will never know what he found. He was not heard from again, and his body was never recovered.

Was it a wild animal or did he get lost and die in the wilderness? Or is it possible, as locals believe, the spirit of Bob did not want trespassers near his resting place or near his treasure?

2
THE KILLEEN WATCHMAN

The original charter of incorporation for the City of Killeen, written in 1882, had provisions that allowed the city to hire both a police force and watchmen as necessary to maintain the peace, safety and harmony of the newly established city.[2]

The watchman, as identified in the city charter, was to be the individual who would be responsible to tour all of downtown Killeen when the local businesses were closed. This individual was to be the man who, after normal business hours, would be responsible for patrolling all of the streets and alleys in the downtown area to ensure there were no drunks passed out in alleys or maybe someone there who had been injured and was in need of assistance. The most important element of his responsibilities was to keep watch in the downtown area for fires that may have started during the long and lonely nights.

Fire was a source of concern to the founding fathers of the City of Killeen because of the widespread use of candles, oil lanterns and later gas lights to illuminate the interiors and exteriors of buildings downtown. As these buildings were built quite close together (most of them shared common walls), a single untended ignition source could easily result in a rapidly expanding conflagration. A fire of this sort at night could potentially have destroyed most of the buildings in downtown Killeen before being contained.

Thus the primary job of the watchman was to be the city's night patrolman, carrying a lantern from street to street and up and down all of the alleys throughout old town Killeen. Some people say he still does.

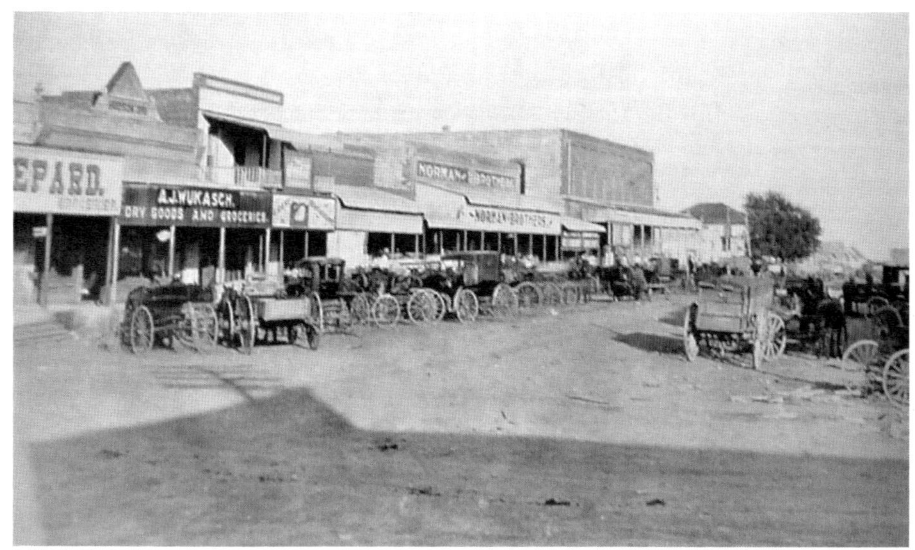

Downtown Killeen, circa 1910.

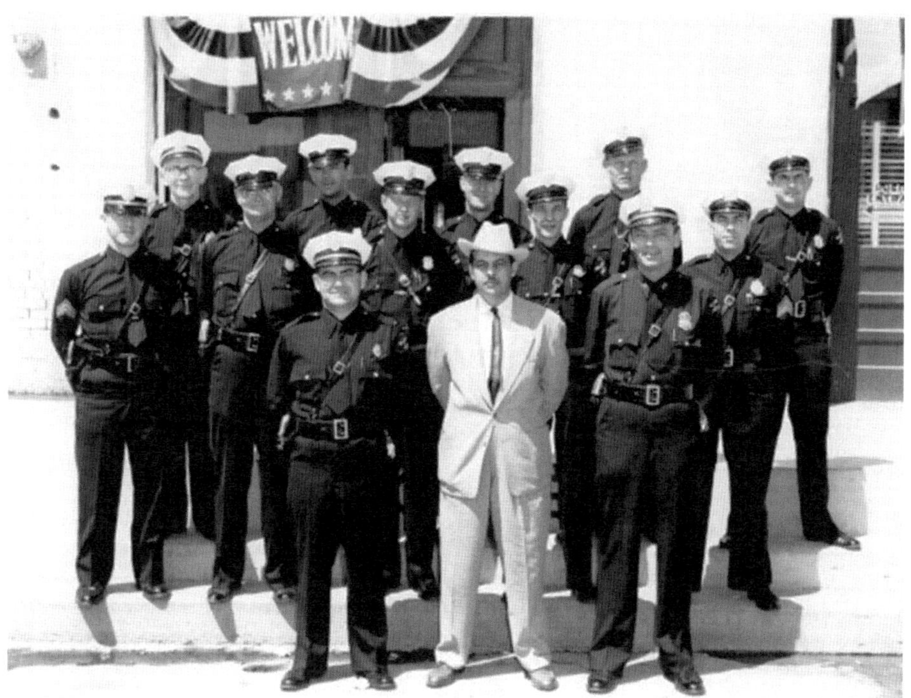

City police force.

Rumor has it that a single watchman was hired by the city back in the late 1800s. The one and only watchman assigned to hold this important position was reported to have faithfully performed his duties for almost thirty long and hard years without fail. But as the city grew larger, it added more police officers to the force. With more police officers, the city was able to provide around-the-clock protection, and the job of the night watchman became superfluous.

The story continues that the city had to let the watchman go after his long and faithful service. In leaving, he was given nothing much more than a hale and hearty handshake and a heartfelt "Well done!" Heartbroken by the loss of his important function, the watchman reportedly died within months of the loss of his employment with the city.

Since then, in the wee early hours of the morning or in the dark of night, lights are often seen moving about in places they shouldn't be in the old historic downtown area of Killeen. The lights that are seen are reported to resemble a lantern, a candle or perhaps even a paranormal orb moving slowly along down Killeen's dark and silent alleys. Logic and reason would say these lights must have been held by someone closing up shop after a long hard day of doing business. Perhaps they were leaving by the back door; maybe they were taking out the last of the day's trash. Or maybe it was just someone who was lost and wandering around in the alley trying to find their way out. More likely it was someone in the alley who was there for a more nefarious purpose like breaking into the closed businesses or spray-painting graffiti on the walls. Each time the lights are reported, the alleys are thoroughly checked out by police officers. Rarely are the lights that were seen tracked down to human origin.

One report was made of a shop owner who was disposing of his last bag of trash in a dumpster in the alley. He observed a light like a lantern moving slowly down the alley toward him. He called out, and it seemed to stop, then started moving sideways toward a wall. Thinking it may have been some young hooligan wanting to spray graffiti on the walls along the alley, he ran toward the light yelling for whoever it was to get out of there.

The light vanished when it reached the side of the alley. When the shop owner got to where it disappeared, he was dumbfounded. There was no door or window on the wall the light had gone toward. It was as if the light and whoever held it had just passed through the solid wall.

With a rapid heartbeat and wobbly knees, the shop owner walked slowly backward to the door of his own business and entered his shop. He swore never ever to go into that alley alone again.

Perhaps the night watchman has decided he has not yet completed his nightly rounds of downtown Killeen. Perhaps the position of responsibility he had held meant so much to him that he continues to patrol the alleyways and streets of downtown Killeen, always on the lookout for fires, ready to call them away and awaken the townspeople to fight and contain the blaze.

3

Tutor Terror

Temple, Texas

In Temple there exists an old unoccupied building. It is a former nursing home that went out of business. As a nursing home, death was common, as residents allegedly passed away from age or other natural causes. But is that what really happened?

One man and his wife were interested in visiting it as he had heard it might be haunted. He and his wife were somewhat fascinated in the paranormal and thought it would be fun to search for ghosts there. With so many people having died there over the decades, they figured it just had to be haunted.

They contacted the people who leased the vacant building, and it turned out the Light Paranormal Investigations was the lessee. They were greeted at the door and invited to tour on their own. They were warned to be careful in the northeast end of the building, as there reportedly was a malevolent presence there.

Undaunted, the ghost hunter and his wife entered that end of the building. The man continued in, but his wife froze on the threshold. Turning back to her, he saw her eyes wide with fright. Knowing she was sensitive to the paranormal, he raced over to her, and gently taking her shaking hand, he turned and led her outside.

With a shaky voice she tried to explain the horror she felt in the building. Not the spirits of the departed residents—something else was present. Even the resident spirits were frightened of it. It was a demon, an entity so evil even ghosts feared to be near it. Her pleas to her husband that he not go back in went unheeded. She removed a protective necklace she always wore and pressed it into her husband's hands.

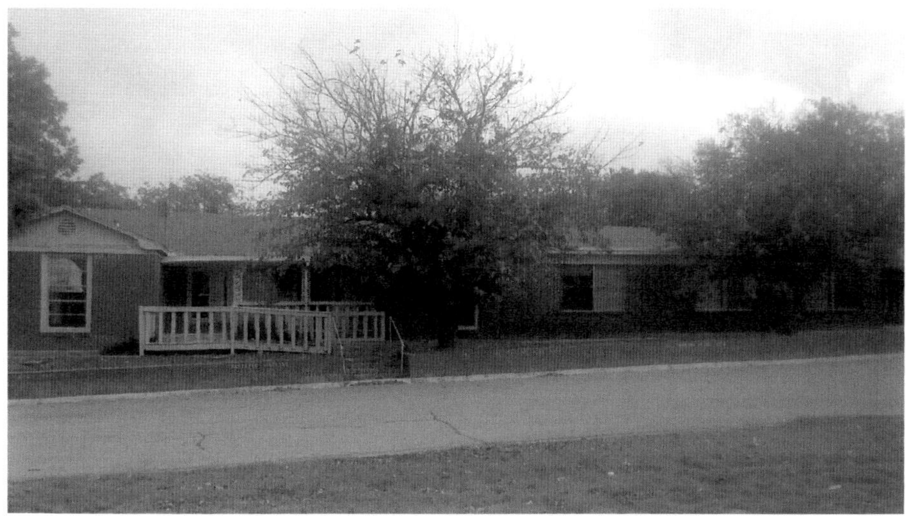

The old Tutor nursing home in Temple.

With a reassuring pat on the side of her face and a smile on his lips, the ghost hunter turned and passed through the entry again. Pulling out a flashlight, he swept it around the hallway. The dust on the furniture and floor were mute evidence of the lack of continuous occupation. Wires were run to cameras in various locations, set up by the paranormal research group.

Seeing nothing out of the ordinary and hearing nothing but his wife's faint pleas that he leave, he proceeded deeper into the murky darkness of the hallway. His flashlight seemed to have trouble penetrating very far down the hall. Banging the flashlight against his hand to fix the problem didn't seem to help.

Knowing he had just installed new batteries, he shook his head in disgust. He made a mental note to buy better batteries next time, not the cheapest he could find. Continuing down the passageway, he strained to see into the shadows cast by his failing light.

He froze as he heard a soft voice saying something indistinguishable. He called out to ask who it was, but the voice continued uninterrupted. It almost sounded as if there were several voices talking at the same time over one another. Cocking his head, he tried to determine where the voices were coming from. It seemed they originated in one of the rooms just ahead of him.

He slowly walked to the doorway and shone his flashlight into the room. Four empty, dusty hospital beds were all he saw. He then decided the voices were not coming from this room, they were coming from down the hall. As he turned to go farther, his light went out, thrusting him into almost total darkness. He banged the flashlight against his hand again, but it stayed dark.

Out of the corner of his eye he saw something glowing down the hall near the ceiling. Turning toward it, he saw two ruby-red eyes glaring at him a short distance away. Shocked and frozen with fear, he heard the soft voices change to a chorus repeating just one word over and over. "Run… Run…Run."

Hurling his flashlight and his wife's necklace at the glowing eyes, he turned and raced back toward the entryway. Running as fast as he could toward the safety of the light outside, he heard a scream of pain from behind him. Slowing only slightly, he glanced behind him. The apparition was writhing on the floor with flames bursting from its hands as it tried to get the necklace off of itself.

Reaching the relative safety outside, he hung his head down and tried to catch his breath. Gasping, he slowly got the story out to his wife. He asked her what the protective necklace was. She told him it was a silver cross that had been dipped in holy water and blessed by a priest.

Catching his breath at last, he went back to the main entrance of the building, and thinking he wouldn't be believed, he told the paranormal researcher they had seen enough and were leaving.

They never went back.

4
The Killeen City Hall Presence

The current city hall was built in 1926 as a brick schoolhouse. It took the place of the 1902 brick city schoolhouse that burned to the ground in a fire in 1922. The current building was built within fifty yards of the original burned-out schoolhouse.

The fire reportedly followed an explosion that was believed to have been caused by coal dust recently delivered to supply the school's furnace to keep the building warm during the winter. The coal was typically delivered down a coal chute located on the side of the building. The delivery process usually created a small cloud of coal dust, and it is believed that the coal dust in the air of the building had accidentally built up in just the right proportions to create a small localized explosive concentration. One spark was all it took.

As the explosion and fire in the original schoolhouse occurred late in the afternoon, no children were known to have been harmed, but it put fear into the hearts of the parents, who realized what could have happened if it had occurred during the school day. The parents had all been told by knowledgeable authorities that brick buildings were not susceptible to fires and did not burn.

Apparently, those same authorities were unaware of the dangers associated with coal dust. It is even possible that these knowledgeable people were some of the same ones who had earlier claimed in 1912 the *Titanic* was not susceptible to flooding and was unsinkable.

The only thing left is a monument standing on the northeast end of the current school's parking lot that memorializes the first brick schoolhouse and the fire that destroyed it.

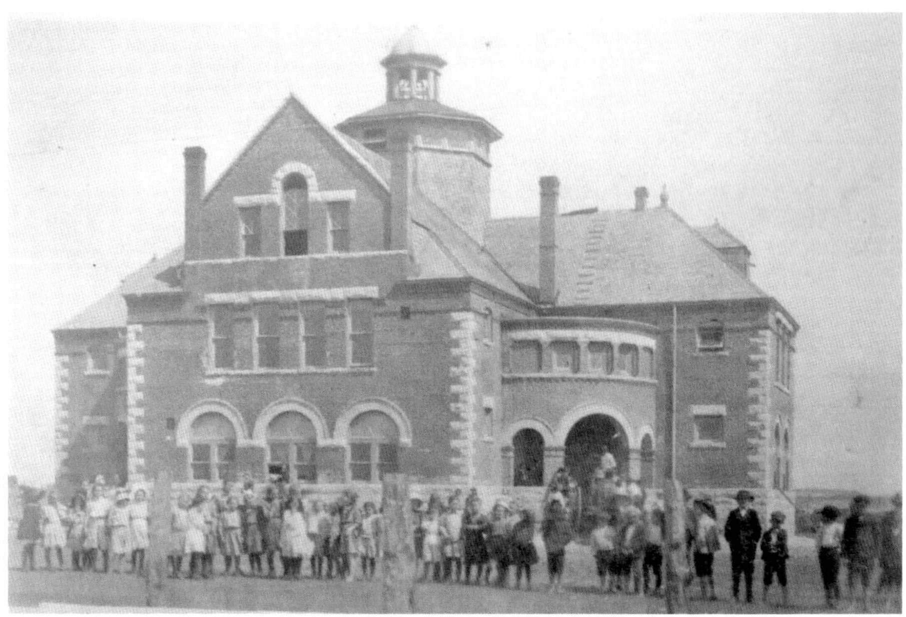

The original Killeen brick schoolhouse, circa 1921.

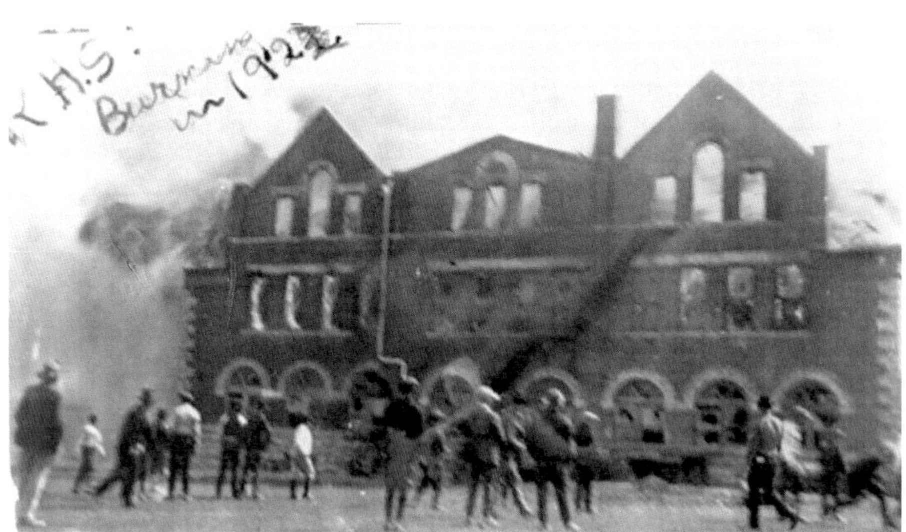

Killeen High School fire, 1923.

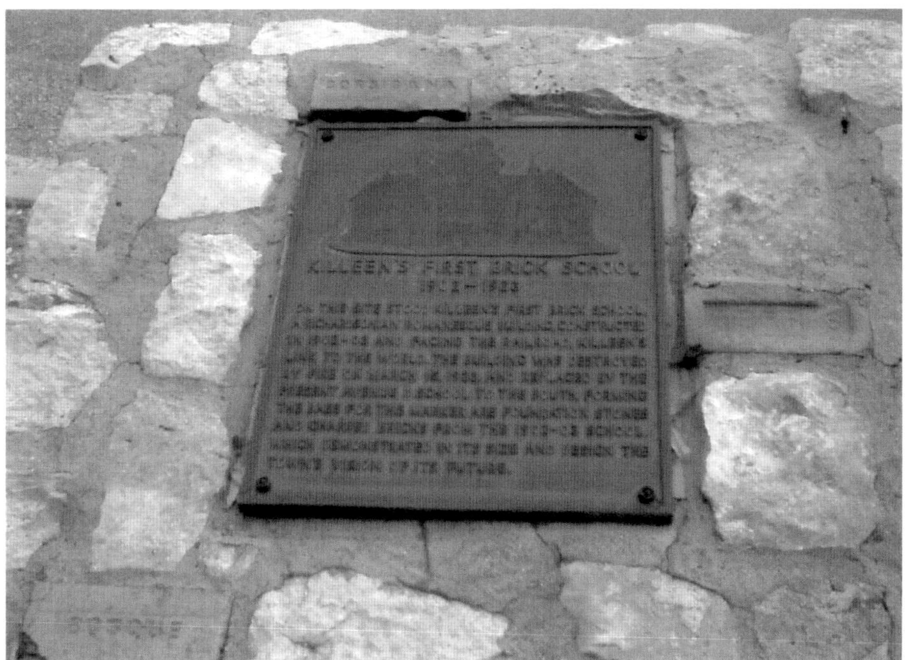

Monument to the original Killeen brick schoolhouse.

City employees rarely come to work very early at the city hall. Let's face it; they are government workers, so there is no real incentive for them to come in early. Some of the rare early birds who have come in to work in the gloomy dark just before sunrise have reportedly experienced unusual and inexplicable occurrences.

None of the employees has reported to have actually sighted an apparition or an entity in the building, but something is known by most to exist there. The eager beaver employees who come in early have occasionally had a sense of discomfort, as if someone or something was following or watching them. An eerie sense of unease pervades the building during the long and lonely nights. The employees report having the hairs on the back of their necks rise and a feeling of dread.

Less frequently, some report the noise of slowly moving furniture within the building, as if someone or something was slowly repositioning some of the chairs or desks. Noises have been heard of office and hallway doors that sound like they are slowly swinging open or closed on their own volition. Footsteps have been heard in halls and on stairs with no one else in the building. It has been reported that people have heard paper rustling in offices as if there were something moving items around on desks. No one else is known to be in the building at that time to be making the sounds being heard. Who or what could be causing the noise? Goose bumps rise on the listener's skin, and the bad feelings build up to a crescendo.

One new employee reported she came in early to work. She was eager to show she was a hard worker and wanted to show her new boss what a great job she could do. The building stood dark and dreary as she approached it. Unlocking and entering, she went to her office area, turned on the light and noticed her coffee cup had been moved to the other side of her desk.

Shrugging it off and blaming the cleaning staff, she sat down and started her computer. As it started up, she noticed movement out of the corner of her eye and heard a rustling sound. She whipped her head around…and saw a piece of paper slowly waving back and forth. She heaved a sigh of relief when she realized the air conditioner had just started up and was blowing air straight on that desk.

Ruefully smiling to herself, she turned back to her monitor. The sound of a door slamming shut behind her caused her to jump to her feet in a panic and whirl around. The door to her supervisor's office was now shut. She was sure it was open when she came in.

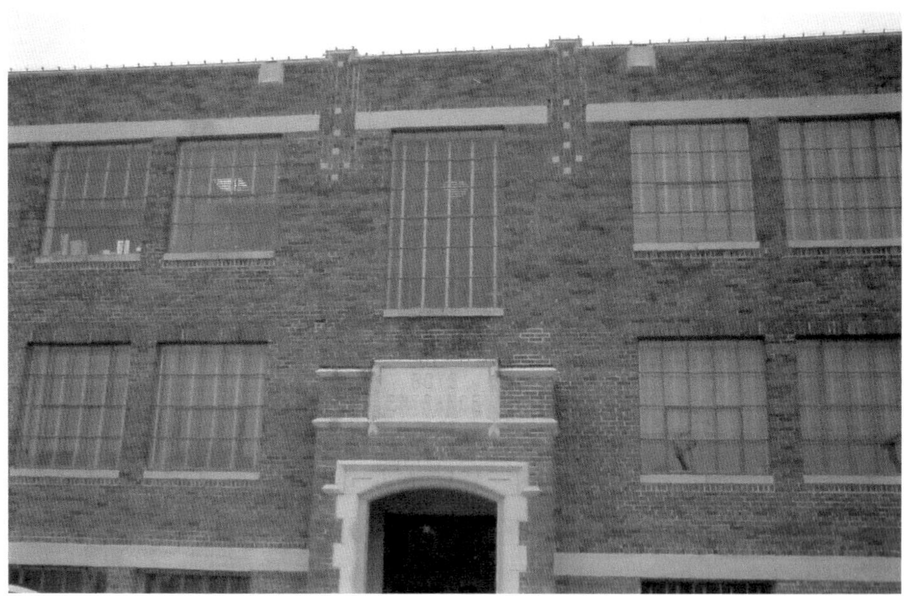

Current Killeen City Hall (Avenue D School built in 1926).

Shaking, she slowly walked over and looked in through the window on the door. Nothing seemed wrong in the office. A loud beep coming from behind her again caused her to jump around. It was only her computer, finally ready to begin a long day of work with her.

She walked over to her desk and leaned down against it. Her hand was beside her coffee cup. The same coffee cup that she had seen on the other side of the desk.

She ran out of the building in a panic and jumped into her car. She sat shaking in her car to await the arrival of other employees.

Other employees also report they wait outside for the arrival of other employees just to reduce their personal discomfort and to provide a sense of safety in numbers when they reenter with other workers.

Could the noises that are heard just be the naturally occurring sounds due to settling or the gentle movement of the building swaying slightly in the wind?

Could the building air conditioning or heater have just been starting up on its regular cycle in the early morning? It has been set to start early to begin cooling or heating the building to improve the conditions within the building for the comfort of daytime employees. Could this simple mechanical operation be causing the doors to move and papers to rustle seemingly without any human intervention?

Could there be rats, bats, mice or other vermin contained within the walls, ceilings and floors that are causing the eerie sounds? Perhaps these foul creatures come out in the dark of night and brush up against the doors, causing them to move. Perhaps it is the scuttling of tiny little feet on the floor that is thought to be paper on desks rustling.

Any of these reasonable and rational scientific explanations are possible, but they do not explain the goose bumps, the sensation of being watched or the feeling of dread that employees have reportedly experienced early in the morning.

Perhaps it is just the spirits of deceased principals, teachers, and students returning to a familiar place to try to re-create a happier and better time in their lives.

Perhaps it is the spirits of former city employees who are returning to work to continue providing service for the citizens of Killeen.

Maybe it will turn out to be a malevolent and evil entity that feeds on the aggravation and irritation the citizens and city workers feel and experience in everyday city operation.

5

Ghosts of the Treasure of the Golden Bull

Salado, Texas

In 1541, while searching for the fabled Seven Cities of Cibola, the former governor of Mexico Francisco Vázquez de Coronado led a group of hundreds of men and over one thousand natives north into the southwestern United States. During his quest, while heading toward what is now New Mexico, Coronado passed through the Brazos basin in Texas. Some say a few of his men may have been left behind or deserted when they heard the natives found gold buried beneath the soil in southern Bell County.

Local lore has it that the Spanish conquistadors forced Native Americans to dig out mountains of gold and silver along the Salado Creek in Bell County. After they melted the gold and silver into bars, it is claimed they kept the treasure at the bottom of Comanche Cave in one or two large chambers carved by native laborers deep within a large limestone hill beside the small river.

The story goes that the much abused natives revolted one night, and the conquistadores were all killed. The treasure, thought to be cursed by the natives, was abandoned. While the conquistadores may have died, that does not mean they have given up protecting the treasure they hid.

Attempts have been made to find the treasure locals believe is still hidden in the hills near Salado, Texas. There is a problem with this treasure-seeking, though. The spirits of the dead conquistadors may still guard the hoard.

People have described having an eerie sense of fear when they travel along the creek. Others claimed to have heard soft voices speaking Spanish and the sound of metal on metal, like chainmail clinking together, as dead Spanish soldiers continue to guard their prized treasure.

Much of the legend surrounds a local Native American who died in a Georgetown hospital at 108 years old. He supposedly lived for over 100 years in a cave near the Salado River and had been reported from time to time to have several bars of gold. He claimed it was part of the treasure-trove buried under the hills near his cave.

After befriending the local in the hospital, in 1957, a treasure seeker entered a small cave in a hill near Salado that the Native American had spoken of. He spent several days wandering the meandering tunnels until he was deep inside the earth. He eventually stumbled into a large cavern with gold and silver bars neatly stacked in rows. The largest single gold piece in the cave was shaped to resemble a golden bull with large red rubies for eyes.

As he feasted his eyes on the fortune, he began to hear things in the cavern around him. He heard the sound of hammers beating on metal, voices softly speaking Spanish in the distance and, increasingly louder, the sound of chainmail clinking against stone.

Panicked, he ran for his life back through the cave he entered. Coming to intersections, he didn't hesitate but plunged madly, trusting in his instinct to guide him back the way he came. After a while, he ran out of steam and paused, leaning a hand against the cold stone wall. Slowly catching his breath, he began to wonder where he was. He had marked the path as he came in, but this section looked like nothing he had encountered. Looking back, he shuddered. He didn't want to retrace his steps for fear he would run into whatever was making the noises.

It took another week for the explorer to find his way out. During that time, he felt the ground shudder and shake several times. Dehydrated and suffering from his experience, he spent eight months in the hospital recovering. Was it just stale air that caused his illness and hallucinations, as scientists would claim, or was it the Spanish conquistadors, continuing to protect their treasure?

When he returned to the treasure-trove, the passages were sealed, collapsed by cave-ins from the small quakes he felt while he was trying to find his way out. Few people believed his claim. Finally, desperate not to be thought of as a liar, he took and passed a lie detector test that confirmed his tale of terror and treasure.

The story of his find came into the spotlight in 1965 as the news was flashed around the country by the United Press. On February 23 and 24, 1965, many newspapers such as the *Bryan Texas Eagle*, the *Brownwood Texas*

Bulletin and even papers as far away as the *Los Angeles Times* carried the news of a huge treasure that had been hidden by the Spanish in southern Bell County, Texas.[3] This created a huge gold frenzy, as others tried to retrace his steps and enrich themselves. Despite years of labor and millions invested in searching, their efforts came to naught. The spirits were not willing to twice reveal the treasure they jealously guard. Many of those searching became ill and believed it to be the ghosts' way of warning them off.

There are still some who claim to hear sounds and Spanish voices softly whispering in the night in the hills by the river, Spanish soldiers speaking softly among themselves and the gentle clink of their armor as they move.

6
HASTINGS HAUNTS

At the southeast corner of W.S. Young and East Veterans Memorial Boulevard stands a large commercial building that has had many unusual and inexplicable occurrences. This prime location was the home for Hastings, a music video and bookstore for over a decade, with a Dollar General occupying a small portion of the building beside it. Prior to the bookstore moving in, the location was the home of a Randall's Food Store.

The food store's employees had reported hearing noises coming from aisles when no one was in them. Coming in early in the morning, the first employees arriving to unlock and open the store would find that cans of food had been stacked up in pyramid shapes in the aisles. Yet no one had been in the store all night.

The strange unexplained noises and occurrences didn't stop when the food store moved out and the bookstore moved in.

The bookstore employees reportedly heard noises in the store when no one else was around. They told of hearing the sound of soft distant footsteps echoing from the back room when no one was supposed to be in there. The night shift workers heard the sound of chairs and desks being scraped across the floor of an unoccupied office after hours on several occasions. Soft distant voices were heard just above the threshold of audibility whispering unintelligible words. Were they spirits speaking a foreign language or just an entity trying desperately to communicate a message or a warning?

Employees complained of materials being moved around behind their backs. They would lay down an object, and when they turn back to use it, it has been repositioned, sometimes across the room. Other times they would see magazines knocked off of the check stands near the front doors. Papers that had been stacked up neatly in the manager's office would be found strewn about the office, and a bone-chilling cold was felt in the air.

Lights were found back on when employees knew for sure they turned them off when they left the room or would turn themselves off when an employee was in the room alone.

The Slushee machine was known to turn itself on and off when no one was anywhere near it and even at night, when no one else was supposed to be inside the building.

Crickets were known to swarm the sides of the building in certain seasons. While this would not seem to be an unusual occurrence (crickets do swarm in certain seasons), they seemed to swarm this store more than others. Perhaps they were attracted to the building because they were attracted to the sounds coming from within it, sounds that were inaudible to the human ear.

Were these supernatural noises and occurrences just a fantasy or the overactive wild imagination of employees left in the darkened building late in the evening when they were all alone or in pairs? Were these noises perhaps just echoes coming from the afterhours workers at the general merchandise store next door? Were other bookstore employees just playing pranks or trying to mess around with the other employees' minds by creating the ghostly noises, repositioning material objects and turning lights on and off? Or is it just possible that these eerie events might be the echoes of former or deceased employees of this company or a previous occupant of the building who still are reporting to work on the graveyard shift?

The bookstore eventually had to move out of this location and into a new larger location on Lowes Boulevard in Killeen. No doubt this was a business decision that was not related to the possible haunting of the old location and the discomfort of the store's employees.

No unusual noises, events or occurrences have been reported yet by employees of the bookstore at the new location, nothing except for the crickets. The crickets no longer swarm around the old location and have taken to swarming around the new building. No one seems to know why.

But the hauntings did not end with the bookstore moving. Even the new occupants have observed strange things happening and have the creeping feeling of unease crawling up their spines.

One manager working late in the evening had the lights in the office go off. When she stood to go to turn them back on, they came back on by themselves. She had heard stories told of someone who had died in that office but had not really believed them. At least she hadn't believed them until then.

Employees reported strange noises they could not identify and merchandise being moved that shouldn't have been.

Another new manager was working late and had to go back into the deepest part of the storage room. As she went back there, she heard something moving around in the clothing merchandise stored there. Calling out, she went to investigate but found there was no one around.

Shaking it off as her imagination, she moved farther into the darker portion of the warehouse. She felt a chill on her arms as if an air conditioner had turned on and was blowing the air straight at her. But there was no movement of the air, just the chill. She stopped moving, and chills ran up and down her spine to match the chill on her arms. Her heart started pounding so loudly she thought it would burst. With her feet frozen in place, she slowly looked around her. Shadows that had previously seemed normal now appeared to be malevolent, containing any sort of evil being.

In a panic, she ran from the warehouse and into her office. She paced back and forth in the office trying to calm down. Her heart rate slowed down, and her hands slowly stopped shaking.

Laughing to herself, she shook her head and passed it off as her overactive imagination. She swore not to watch scary movies before coming to work ever again. Then she glanced at the security monitor showing the back of the warehouse. Her eyes glued to the monitor, she slowly picked up the intercom and requested another employee to come to the office.

When the other employee arrived, she asked what her boss wanted. The manager simply pointed to the security monitor. Moving around the desk, she looked and, gasping, looked again.

There on the screen that showed the unlit warehouse were floating orbs—orbs of light that were slowly drifting about within the darkened warehouse. Some of the orbs moved faster, some moved slower, a couple even seemed to be playfully chasing each other around.

Ever so slowly, the orbs moved offscreen or in among the merchandise where they could not be seen on the monitor.

The manager stopped the recording disc and moved it back to see it again. There was only static shown on the screen with a date and time stamp. She tried moving back to earlier in time. She watched herself go into the storeroom, stop and run out. The screen showed only static after that.

Did they just imagine what they had seen on the screen? Or was the back room really still haunted?

7
Marshal's Office Menace

The color video monitor showed nothing more than the normal view of the city marshal's office. It was afterhours on a normal workday, and that office was unoccupied. The person working in the room with the monitor wished he was home, but a city employee's work was never really done. He bent down over more of the tedious paperwork that overflowed his inbox.

The city marshal's office was formerly one of the city banks. Its vault and teller area were converted to house the marshal's office.

Motion on the screen caused the employee to glance over at it. None of the marshals were supposed to be in the building that late. He peered intently at the screen but could discern nothing out of the ordinary. He shivered as if cold, and a trickle of sweat slowly made its way down his spine. He shrugged at the apparent motion he had noticed as just his overactive imagination and turned back to his work.

More movement caught the corner of his eye. Swiftly jerking his head to look at the screen, his blood froze as he saw a shadow of a figure start to cross the office. Shaking his head to clear his eyes, he stared intently at the screen, but where the figure had been, nothing was left but a desk and chair, the same table and chair that had always been there. Nothing looked disturbed or out of place. Still, he could have sworn he had seen something, something moving in that office.

Turning ruefully back to his work, he slowly shook his head in disbelief. There were no such things as ghosts, it was just his imagination. He was tired

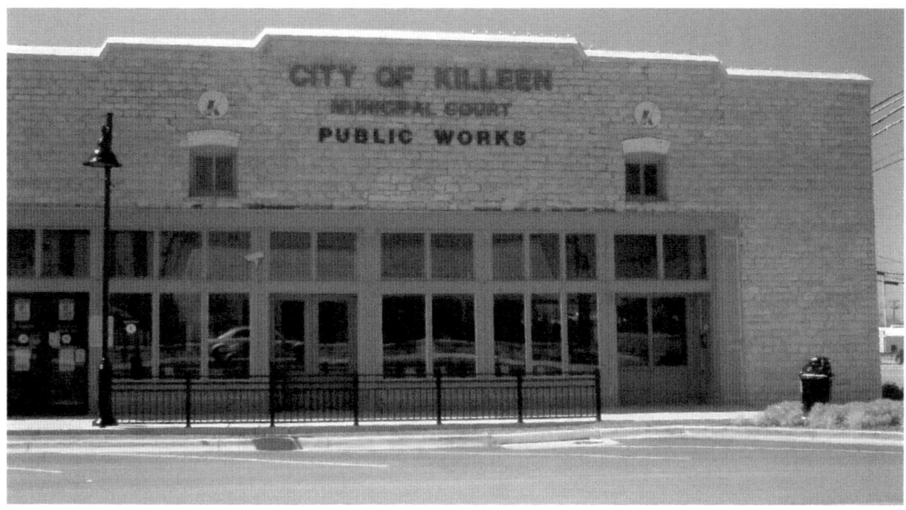

Location of the marshal's office in Killeen.

of all of his dreary work and thought maybe he was just getting tired. He stretched his aching back and rubbed his weary eyes. One more case file and he'd call it a night.

Once again, he felt a shiver run down his spine, goose bumps appeared on his arms and the hair rose. A feeling of dread slowly came over him. The office felt cold, colder than it should have. Slowly, he turned back to the monitor showing the view of the marshal's office. The shadow he thought he had seen was back, but much clearer and more substantial this time. While it was a color monitor, the figure appeared to be in black and white. It was a figure of a woman wearing a bustle dress from the 1900s and carrying an open parasol over her shoulder. She moved slowly across the monitor and entered into the vault.

His heart raced as he watched the apparition vanish into the vault area. He stared at the monitor, waiting for the image to reappear, but to no avail.

He picked up the phone to call for the police to investigate the room but realized before he finished dialing how it would sound if nothing was found there. He could not afford to be thought of as the crazy city employee who saw things that weren't there. He slowly lowered the phone onto its cradle and considered what he should do.

Getting up, he looked around for an improvised weapon. He saw an umbrella he kept for emergencies, grabbed it up and started for the door. The umbrella might not do any harm to a ghost, but it wasn't likely there was a ghost in the marshal's office—more likely it was someone who had been inadvertently locked in when the rest of the employees went home. Besides, it gave him the feeling that he had at least something to defend himself with in case the person was upset at being locked in. One last look at the monitor showed the spirit had returned. She stood facing the vault, and then she slowly looked over her shoulder at the video camera. In horror, he looked deeply into the soulless, black and empty eyes resting in the bones of a human skull.

He stared at the screen in horror as she again moved into the vault. Panicking, he grabbed for the phone. But what could he tell the police emergency dispatcher? If he said he had seen a ghost, they would just laugh at him. No one would believe him ever again.

Deciding to get proof of the spirit, he picked up his cellphone and activated the video camera function. He left his office and moved quietly through the courtroom. He paused at the marshal's door and listened for any sound that might be coming from within. The only sound he heard was the pulsing of his heartbeat pounding in his ears.

He keyed in the combination on the keypad and gently pushed the door open. Peeking around the corner, he saw the office appeared deserted. He advanced slowly into the empty room with the umbrella held over his shoulder like a club, fully prepared to race back the way he came if anything happened.

Just as he reached the desk, the umbrella sprang open, startling him. Tossing the open umbrella over the desk, he dove back through the door. Lying on his back in the courtroom, he stared fearfully back at the room, terrified of what might be there. Seeing nothing but the open umbrella rocking on the desk, he slowly rose to his feet and brushed himself off. Reviewing his actions mentally, he thought he must have gripped the umbrella too tight and inadvertently pressed the button on the umbrella himself, causing it to open.

Returning to the door, he reentered the room with a little less trepidation. Striding over to the desk, he recovered his umbrella and closed it. Looking around, he could see nothing out of the ordinary in the office. Still, a shiver again ran down his spine as he looked at the vault door. Creeping over, umbrella and camera in hand, trembling only slightly, he slowly peered around the door frame and gazed into the vault. Nothing but filled file cabinets stared back. He cautiously entered the vault and, peeking behind the cabinets, found nothing amiss. A noise emanating from the office behind him startled him. While throwing himself forward to safety behind a file cabinet, he violently slashed back behind him with his sword-like umbrella.

The phone in the marshal's office rang again.

Sheepishly, he pulled himself out from behind the file cabinet and left the vault. The phone stopped ringing before he could reach it. He moved about the office, looking for any other sign of the spirit having passed through, but there was nothing there. Nothing but the memory of those eyes, those hauntingly empty eyes that appeared to burn a hole into his soul and gave him chills every time he thought of them.

8
Killeen Firehouse Activity

The Killeen Fire Department was founded in 1920 as a volunteer fire department. In the 1920s, it had several homes along Gray Street for its limited equipment. After the brick schoolhouse on College Street in downtown Killeen burned to the ground, the city moved to hire full-time firefighters to supplement the volunteers. The city also erected a building at 114 West Avenue D to house the ever increasing amount of firefighting equipment it was purchasing.

This fire station is no longer used to house young firemen. Perhaps the reason it is no longer in use is because it is reported to be possessed. Over the years, many firefighters have had experiences with a paranormal entity within. They have reported unusual sounds that have been heard in the building late in the evenings and at night.

One firefighter reported he was going down the stairs to retrieve a phone he had left in a fire engine. He did not think he had to use the stairwell light because he had worked there so long that moving through the building was just second nature for him. Besides, he thought the light from outside the firehouse provided adequate illumination for so simple a task.

As he neared the bottom of the stairs, he heard the creaking of the metal entrance door opening. Looking that way, he saw the door was still shut. Freezing in place, he then heard the noisy sound of the metal door slowly shutting. His heart started racing as he heard the noisy sound of boots starting up the stairs in front of him.

In a panic, he ran up the stairs and into the break room. Several of the firemen watching the television gave him strange looks. They thought he was white as a sheet, as if he had seen a ghost. How little they knew how close they came to the truth. In a shaky voice, he told them of what happened on the stairwell.

Being he-men types (just ask one), they ran out of the break room to check it out. Turning on the stairway light and going down the stairs, they found nothing amiss. There were no noises, and the entrance door was securely shut.

Laughing at the scaredy-cat, they started back up the stairs. They stopped as they heard the distant sound of a fire bell ringing. Then there came the sound of boots pounding down the stairs through them.

From the bay below them came the distant sound of the bay doors opening and of horses whinnying, stomping and straining at ancient harnesses, as if readying to haul an old-fashioned fire wagon to the scene of a fire in town. The hoof beats rose into a crescendo and then slowly faded away into the distance.

They all agreed never to speak of it again. It never happened. It couldn't have happened. So it didn't.

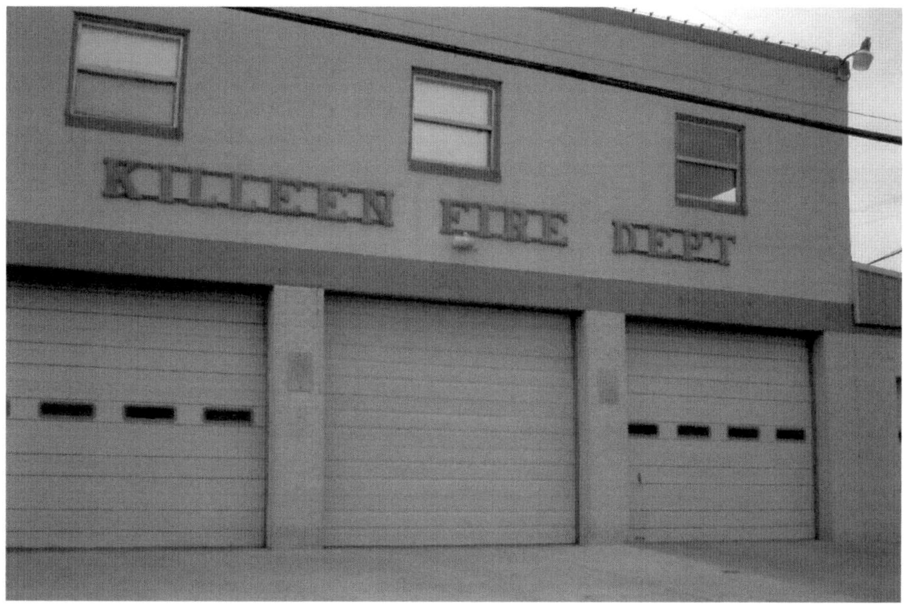

The original Killeen fire station at 114 West Avenue D.

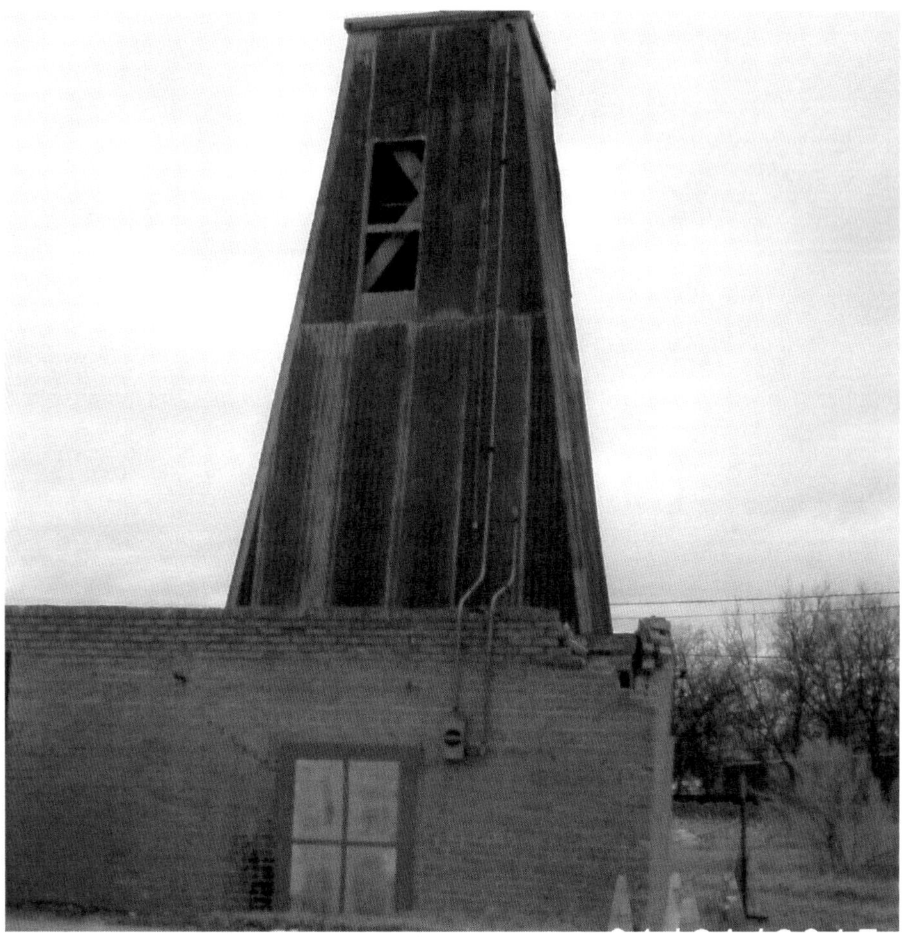

The building housing the original Killeen City well.

Another startling story told of this firehouse includes firemen sound asleep in their upstairs bunks late one night. The fire alarm went off, alerting the men of the need to man their truck.

Jumping into their heavy boots and pulling up their bunker gear, they raced to their truck…and realized there was no alert. There was no sound of the alarm bell ringing, and the lights in the break room and stairwell had not come on automatically as they normally would in an actual alarm callout. Looking around at one another, they sheepishly shrugged and went back upstairs to go back to bed.

They froze in place when the sound of the engine of one of the trucks started up in the bays below them. The duty driver raced down the stairs to see who was messing with his engine. To his shock, there was no one sitting in the cab who could have pressed the ignition button and started the engine. The engine slowly wound down and died.

Going slowly back up to the bunkroom in silence, they lay down in their bunks. None of them slept the rest of the night, listening intently for the sounds of whatever spirits had possessed their truck and fire station.

Behind the firehouse stands the original well, built around 1914, that supplied all of the water needs of the city in its infancy. Strange floating lights have been observed moving around the base of the dilapidated building, but no one is there when it is investigated. Are these orbs the restless spirits of deceased residents or just the overactive imaginations of the locals?

9
BISTRO MALEVOLENCE

In a small building on the southwest corner of Gray and East Avenue D in Killeen sits the town's newest and most elite fine-dining bistro. Gourmet food galore is served to discriminating customers during the light of day. But at night, a different type of customer arrives with different desires, one with paranormal powers and an appetite for harassing the employees.

Late at night, when employees are trying to clean up after a hard day of serving customers, they have reported strange things happening. Noises when there should be none, items moved around seemingly of their own volition, feelings of apprehension and dread and, finally, actual attacks on the helpless workers.

The building itself was originally constructed as a bank. The First National Bank was a place where the citizens of the city of Killeen and the surrounding communities could place their money in confidence. The building was a relatively late addition to the booming city, having been built in 1907, right after the turn of the century. With a modern vault (for the time) with walls over a foot thick, it was considered to be a relatively safe place to store people's hard-earned money.

The bank moved on, and the building went through several other tenants over the years, including a dress shop front purportedly for a gambling establishment. Finally, it was turned into a restaurant. The first restaurant that decided to occupy the newly furnished restaurant was Tank's Pub.

A former worker reported things just weren't right there. She reported a general feeling of uneasiness or apprehension. When she put out condiments

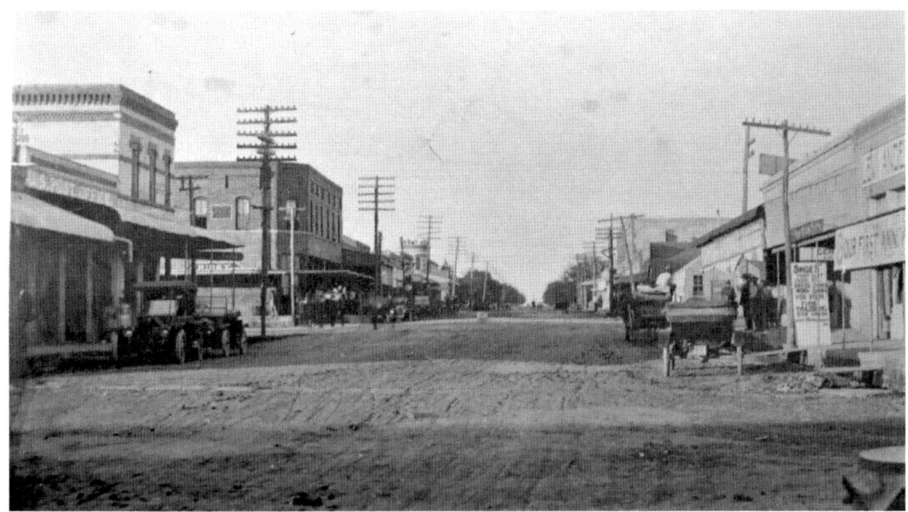

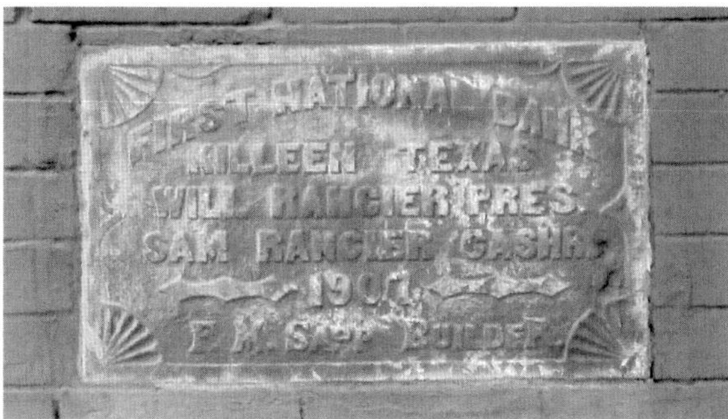

Above: Looking North on Gray Street in Killeen (Sixth Street at the time of the photo), circa 1910.

Left: First National Bank building at 224 East Avenue D in Killeen, built in 1907.

on tables and stepped away for a minute, they were sometimes rearranged when she came back. Sometimes, they were not even on the same table she had put them on.

In the back, pool balls were slowly rolled across tables by themselves. Of course, this could have been just a slightly uneven floor or unlevel table. Or maybe the fan for the heater or air conditioner kicked on and gave the balls just enough impetus to start their slow roll across the table.

The fan coming on or the unlevel building could not explain the soft echo of footsteps that were sometimes heard coming from the second floor. The second floor was not accessible from the interior of the building but was where equipment and supplies were stored.

Citing a downturn in business due to the streets being torn up during a prolonged downtown revitalization, Tank's Pub moved a few blocks away to set up on Veterans Memorial Boulevard.

The new restaurant to move in was Scratch Elevated Bistro. As it turns out, the entity may not have moved out with Tank's Pub. No, it seems the entity may have been anchored to the building and was not yet through with its mischievous machinations.

Alone late one night, a manager was cleaning up after closing. She felt uneasy, as if someone were watching her. Looking around, she spotted the security cameras. Laughing, she chided herself for being skittish and turned back to her work.

She froze when she heard soft footsteps coming from the second floor. There wasn't supposed to be anyone else in the building, especially anyone up there with the supplies.

Slowly, she moved over to the front door, doing her best to move noiselessly. She gently turned the knob on the door. It was still locked.

Knowing no one could have gotten in that way, she grabbed a baseball bat she kept behind the bar for just such an occasion, went outside and unlocked the gate on the door to the second floor.

She softly crept up the stairs, clutching the bat as if it was a life preserver and she was stranded in the ocean. She reached the second floor and started down the hall.

The unfettered light from the streetlights outside gave a ghastly glow to the interior. With trembling hands and a heart ready to pound its way out of her chest, she stuck her head around doorways to look for whomever—or whatever—had been making the noise.

Nothing was there.

Sighing with relief, she went back to the stairs and started down. Suddenly, she felt a gentle push from behind. Stumbling, she grabbed the handrail and prevented a nasty fall. Jumping down the stairs three at a time, she reached the bottom and looked back up the stairs, bat in hand, ready to swing. Again, nothing was there. Shaking her head, she laughed softly. Her imagination must really be working overtime. She relocked the gate to the second floor and went back inside the bistro.

She ensured the door behind her was locked and walked back over to the bar to put the bat away. As she leaned down, she felt a swish of air pass by her ear. She jerked her head up just in time to see an Irish coffee glass shatter against a nearby table.

Looking up to the shelf that held the coffee glasses, she saw one was missing. As she watched with incredulous eyes, another Irish coffee glass began rocking back and forth, faster and faster.

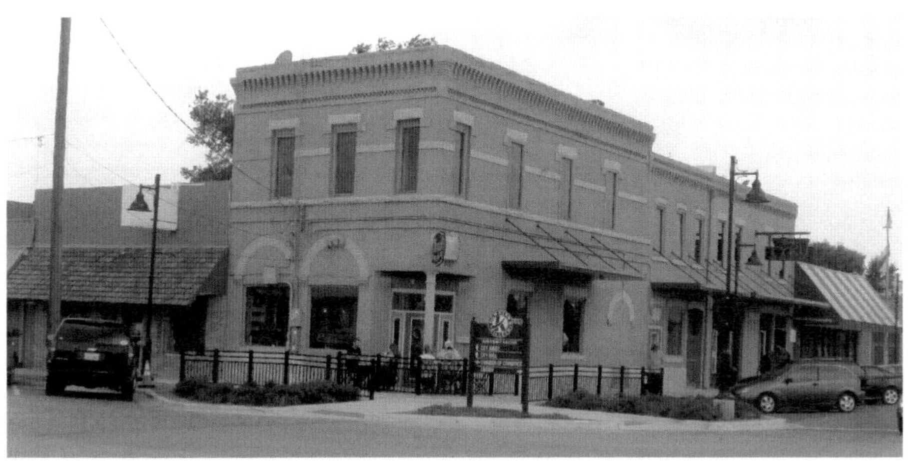

224 East Avenue D in Killeen.

In horror, she ran to the front door and slammed into it. It was locked! She hastily unlocked it, threw it open and ran out into the night.

Standing beside her car, she watched the bistro for a while. Slowly, her heartbeat crept back to somewhere close to its normal rate. Her hand shook as it held the latch of her car door. The front door to the bistro was closed. But she had opened it when she left.

As cautiously as a nervous cat in a roomful of rocking chairs, she crept back to the front door and locked it. She may have been terrified of the supernatural, but she was still a responsible manager and the boss counted on her a lot. She hurtled back to her car and raced away. Cleanup could wait until daylight.

There are always those who doubt the existence of spirits. One of those doubting Thomases was a co-worker at the bistro. She couldn't believe glasses could just throw themselves at people. As she helped clean one evening, she scoffed that perhaps the other worker had been sampling too much of the alcohol in the bar.

She doubted until an Irish cream glass hurtled at her unprotected back, striking her violently and causing her to collapse on the floor. In pain, she whipped her head around to see who could have thrown something at her. All of her co-workers were working at the other end of the bistro with her. No one was near the bar where the glasses were stored on shelves.

She doubts no more.

She ended up with a large bruise on her upper back and a new respectful regard for paranormal entities.

10
THE RAILROAD ENTITY

For many years, a deteriorated building stood just north of the railroad tracks on the east side of College Street in downtown Killeen. Old and broken down, it was the epitome of what a haunted house should look like. Word on the street was that it was haunted, and no one in town really wanted anything to do with it. Originally built in the late 1800s to support railroad operations for the trains that ran through Killeen, the unoccupied support building slowly deteriorated as the rail traffic through the area diminished.

Lights were seen flickering and floating around inside the building in the deepest darkest part of the night. The sounds of banging, hammering and sawing were heard repeatedly. But when railroad employees arrived the next morning to investigate, no one was found in or near the building and nothing within appeared to have been disturbed.

The building was finally torn down when railroad management determined it was an unattractive nuisance and too much of a potential liability. But the paranormal spirit that occupied the building was not to be appeased by the mere destruction of the building it had inhabited for so long.

With the building it occupied gone, the spirit was free to wander about the area searching for another more permanent anchor. People occupying the surrounding buildings have reported mysterious occurrences over the years. Strange, inexplicable noises in the evening, papers and furniture found moved about, no one is sure what it is that the entity seeks.

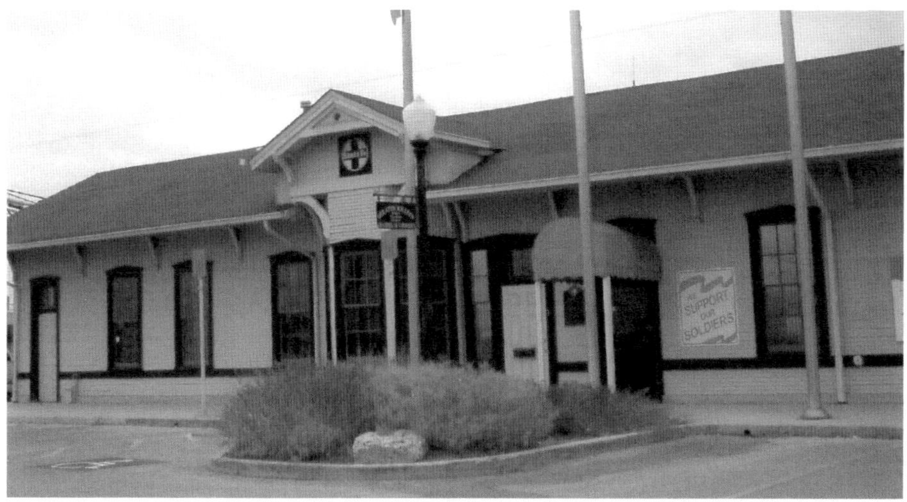

Photo of the 1913 Santa Fe Railroad Depot in Killeen.

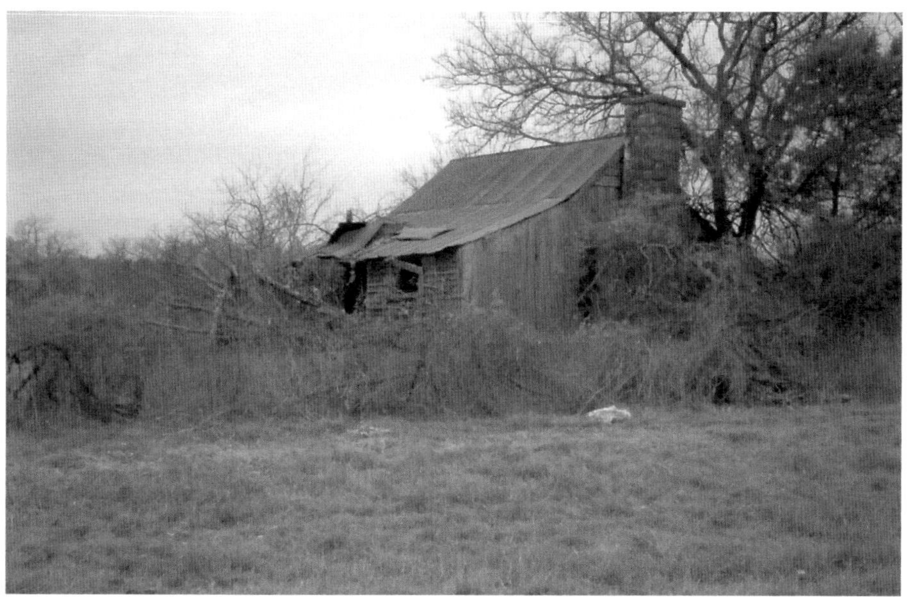

An old deteriorated building (similar to the one torn down).

Was it the spirit of one of the railroad workers trying to continue the difficult task of ensuring proper and timely railroad operations? Was it the Killeen Watchman, preparing for his nightly patrol?

Could it have been the ancient spirits of Native Americans buried on that particular spot and disturbed in their endless slumber by the coming of the railroad?

No one knows the answer. The only thing that they know for sure is that the entity exists.

11

WEDEMEYER WRAITHS

Belton, Texas

In the town of Belton lies an old building. In 1881, the Wedemeyer family moved in and established the Wedemeyer Belton Academy for boys. It was there that Professor Charles Wedemeyer taught until the academy moved to Temple in 1912. The home survived the period between the mid-1800s and early 1900s known as "Bloody Bell County" due to the frequency of bloodshed.[4]

Many are the stories told of the building and the spirits that inhabit it. Multiple intruders were reported to have been shot there during its long and bloody history. Is it possible that some of their spirits or those who shot them still remain, tied to the building of violence, unable to find a permanent peaceful place of rest?

One evening, long after the academy had been closed, a neighbor taking a walk happened to pass the locked, unoccupied former boys' academy. As he came abreast of it, he happened to glance up. He was shocked to see a young girl in a white dress staring back at him from behind gauzy drapes in a second-floor window. Knowing that no one was living there and being concerned for her safety, he called out to her. He watched as she slowly parted the curtain and appeared to say something. Cupping his ear, he pantomimed not being able to understand what she was saying.

She glanced back over her shoulder and, looking like she was terrified at what she saw, let the curtains drop back across the window. She flung her arm across her eyes and leaped back away from the window, out of the neighbor's sight.

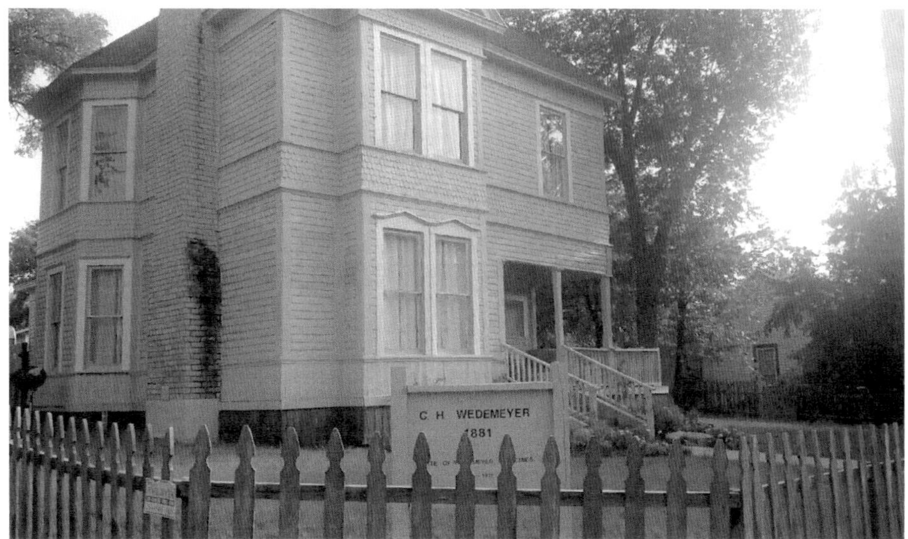

The old Wedemeyer Academy in Belton.

The neighbor was stunned for a moment, taking a few seconds to process what he had seen. Making a decision, he ran up to the house, banged on the door and tried the knob. It was locked. He ran around the building to try to open the back door, but it was boarded up. He next tried each window around the residence, but they, too, were locked from the inside.

Racing back to his house, he found a claw hammer and ran back to rescue the girl. He forced the boarding off the back door and pushed his way into the building. Calling out, he heard no response. He saw a lot of undisturbed dust on the floor. He found a staircase and went upstairs to the room he had seen her in earlier. It was empty. Looking down at the floor near the window she had stood in, he could find no footprints. The only thing visible was years of undisturbed dust buildup.

Thinking he had gone to the wrong room, he searched the rest of the rooms upstairs but found nothing. There was no evidence to show a little girl had ever been inside the home. Shaken, he turned away and slowly descended to the first floor. He cautiously walked around that floor, but there were many years of undisturbed dust with no footprints but his own.

He returned to the back door and closed it, hammering back into place the plywood sheet he had removed to gain entry. He walked back around front to go home. Glancing back one last time, he was startled to see a small dog looking back at him from the window in which he had previously seen the girl. Closing his eyes and shaking his head to clear it, he looked again. The dog was gone.

Thinking for sure there was something going on up there, he returned to the residence, opened the back door and again proceeded upstairs. Once again, he found no prints in the dust other than his own. He went to the window and looked outside. Nothing seemed out of place. He parted the gauzy curtains as he had seen the young girl do but froze as he felt a sudden chill run through him. Dropping the curtains, he looked behind him. Nothing was there but the closed door to the room. Then he realized he had left the door open when he entered.

With trembling feet, he slowly moved back to the doorway and opened the door. He stared in horror as he watched the door across the hallway open just as his did. His pulse racing and goose bumps covering his body, he flung the door fully open and stood staring in horror at his doppelganger, something that looked exactly like him. He was paralyzed with fright as he saw the apparition had the exact same features as him, was wearing the same clothes he wore and stood in the doorway looking back at him with a look of abject terror on its face.

Coming to his senses, he realized he was looking at a mirror, a mirror hung on the wall opposite his door. He grabbed the doorknob and hung on tight as he almost passed out with relief. His knees sagged, and he slowly slid down the door to rest on the floor. He felt a wet warmth between his legs and, looking down, realized he must have wet himself slightly in his fear. He felt like laughing and was glad he had worn dark jeans that day to hide his embarrassment.

Pulling on the doorknob, he stood up and proceeded back down the stairs. He boarded the back door and left for his house. Looking back one last time, he saw a woman in the same window he had seen the girl and dog.

He raced back to his own home as if demons were chasing him. While he eventually began walking the neighborhood again, his walks thereafter never took him past the old Wedemeyer Academy.

12
Morgue Materializations

Few who are not City of Killeen employees know of the presence that inhabits the building that used to be known as the old city morgue. Fewer still know the location of that morgue was the old stone building located at 200 East Avenue D in historic downtown Killeen.

Originally built as a bank at the turn of the century, it was converted to other uses over the years, including a bank, a morgue, city hall, a finance center, water utility collections and, finally, the Killeen Municipal Court. Throughout it all, strange occurrences were noted by the employees diligently working within.

Employees have reported for many years that something just wasn't right in the old stone building. Reports came in of hearing the voices of people who weren't there, sounds of soft footsteps when no one else was in the building, doors that would slowly move without human intervention, a general feeling of unease and sickness among the employees, a feeling of anticipation or sometimes a feeling of being watched and, in one case, a shadow seen dashing between rooms. Cold chills are routinely felt running up and down the spines of the unsuspecting employees. While most of these reports have been made by employees of the city working in the building, others have come from those visiting on business.

One location in particular is known for odd smells and the ill health of the occupant. Many have used that same room, and almost all of them have reported deteriorating physical health. One employee reported she would never again work late in the evening alone in that building after observing something she refused to speak of to her superiors.

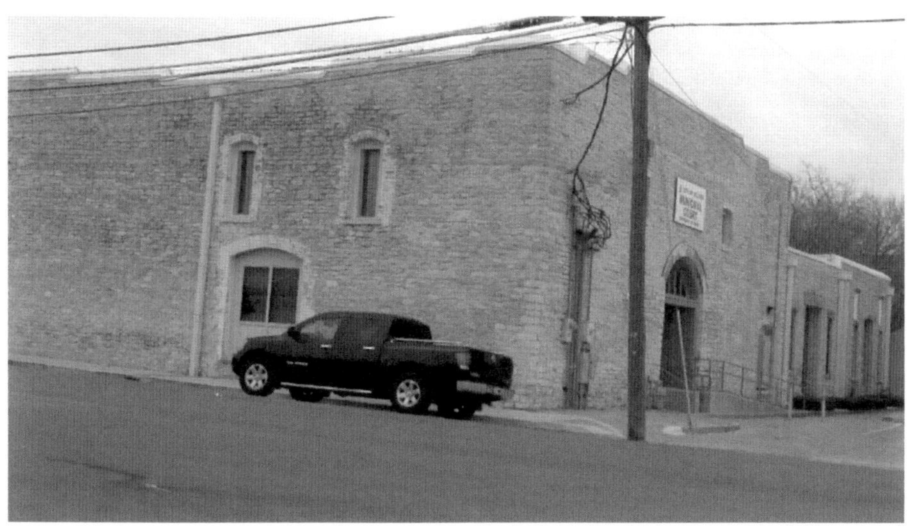

Alleged location of the original City of Killeen Morgue.

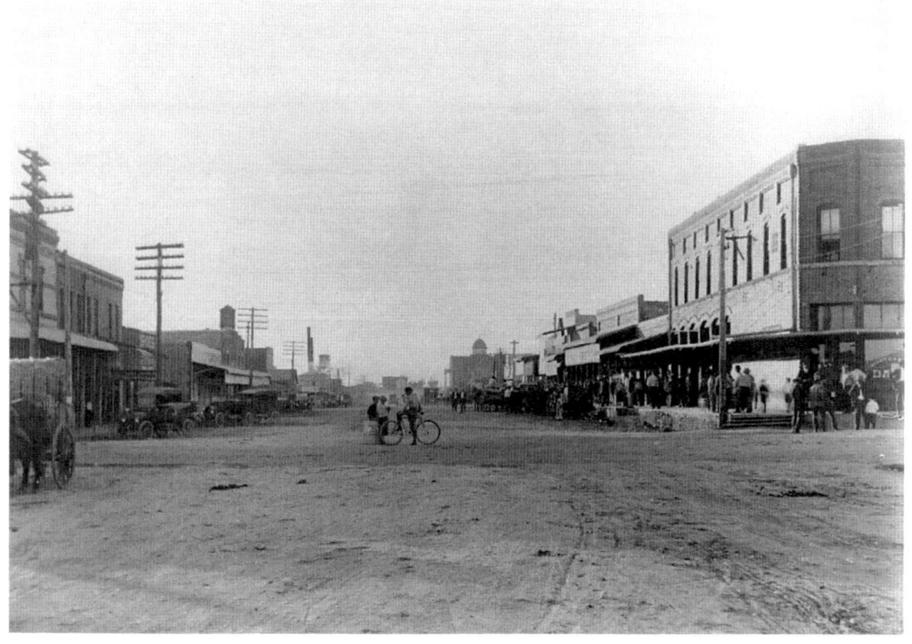

View of Avenue D area in Killeen, circa 1910.

As a fairly new employee trying to make a good impression, she was diligently working late at her desk catching up on documents that had piled up after the departure of her predecessor. She felt a cold chill run up and down her spine as she typed on the keyboard of her computer. She put on a sweater, thinking it was only a typical winter chill.

She heard the soft creaking noise of a door slowly opening in the hall outside her office. Leaving her desk, she went out into the corridor and called out to see who else was in the building. When no one answered, she shrugged her shoulders and went back in to work.

Back at her keyboard, she felt a feathery touch on the back of her neck and whipped around to see who was messing with her. No one was there. Shaking her head, she decided she had imagined it.

She heard a clicking noise come from beside her, as if the key of her electric tabulating calculator had been pushed. Glancing over, she watched as different keys slowly moved down, clicking as they reached the bottom and a number appeared on the paper tape roll above. Frozen with fear, she could only watch helplessly as more keys were pushed. Then the keys on her keyboard started being depressed. Her eyes moved slowly back to the screen of her computer, and she saw the word that had been written. It was only one.

RUN

Springing out of her chair, she ran from of the room in a panic. She didn't stop until she was in her car with the doors locked. Still shaking in fear, she slowly calmed down, started the car and drove home.

When she returned the next morning, there were no numbers on the paper roll of the calculator, and the word she had seen written on her screen was gone. How could she possibly explain to her boss and co-workers what happened to her without being ridiculed?

Was it only that she was overworked, overly tired or maybe had watched too many scary movies? Was it all just her imagination? She did not stay in her new position long, leaving the city and unable to explain the real reason why to her boss and co-worker.

Are the lonely spirits of the dearly departed still walking the halls or patiently inhabiting the same rooms in which they lay for days waiting for burial? Or is it possible that all of the current and former employees reporting the manifestations just imagined the paranormal activity?

13
Maintenance Mystery

The City of Killeen building maintenance shop is located at 2404 East Rancier in Killeen. It is conveniently located right beside the City Cemetery—convenient at least for the restless spirits of those that have passed, those that wander the local area searching for a better location to inhabit.

Employees have reported manifestations inside the maintenance building, ghostly presences that they had personally witnessed or had heard about from former city employees.

Most reported an eerie feeling when they worked late in the building alone. The hairs rising up on their skin and the backs of their necks, a feeling of impending dread or doom was what most reported. And all reported the feeling that they were not alone, that someone was there watching them. But when they looked around, no one else was in the building.

One reported he was working on cutting boards that were going to be used in one of the city buildings the next day. Prior to starting to cut the wood, he ensured the door to the paint locker was closed. This ensured that wood dust would not get into any of the cans of paint. Going back to start cutting, he glanced up and noted the door to the locker was open.

Shaking off the creepy feeling he had been feeling that evening, he decided he hadn't closed it well enough and it must have just slipped open. He went over to the door and pulled it firmly shut this time. He then pulled and pushed on it several times to ensure it had really latched.

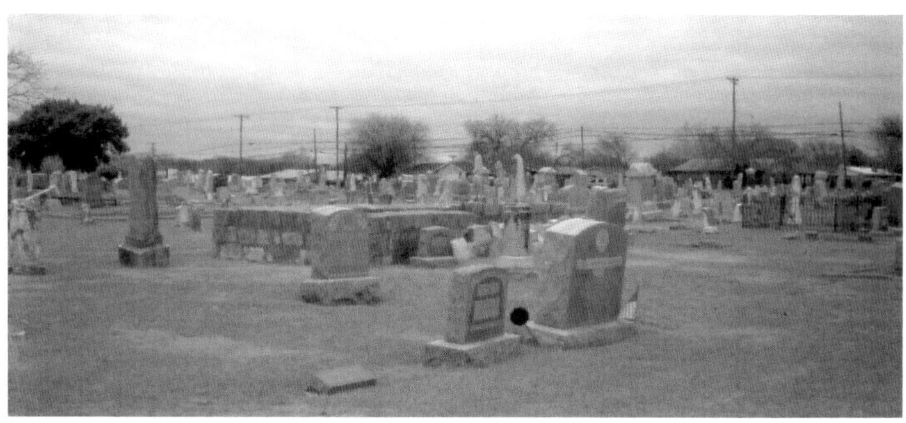

City of Killeen Cemetery.

Going back across the room to the table saw, he placed a wooden board on the table and reached down to start the saw. Glancing up again just before starting, he froze in place. His eyes widened, and his heart started beating rapidly. He could not believe his eyes.

The door was standing wide open. And now, a dark shadow was being cast on the door from the light shining above his head. Nothing was between the light bulb and the door to cast the shadow he saw.

Yelling, he turned and dashed for the door. Tripping on some wood, he fell forward and slammed the door to the building open with his shoulder and rolled out onto the wood-surfaced entryway.

Rapidly picking himself up off the floor, he raced to his car, dove in and peeled out of the parking lot. As he sped along, he told himself over and over that he would never work in that building alone at night again.

14
MAXDALE BRIDGE AND CEMETERY

The Maxdale Bridge was built in 1914 as a major passage across the Lampasas River. It continued to be the primary path across the river until the completion of a new, modern bridge almost ninety years later. The Maxdale Cemetery is located a few hundred yards south of the bridge and is the oldest cemetery in Bell County. It sits on a small rise, providing the deceased a good view of the Lampasas River and the bridge.

Apparitions and ghosts have been sighted both at the bridge and within the cemetery.

Visitors tell of feelings of apprehension and dread that fill them as they traverse the rickety old bridge or venture into the confines of the old cemetery.

Many tales and stories are told of the Maxdale Bridge. Stories tell of the jilted lovers who, in desperation, raced their vehicles to the Maxdale Bridge and attempted to commit suicide by leaping off the side into the roaring torrent of the river raging below.

This endeavor was rarely successful, as it was less than a thirty-foot drop to the slowly moving shallow river below, but their intentions were understood.

Rumor has it that depressed unsuccessful homesteaders hanged themselves from the support structure (or others were hanged for alleged wrongdoings or perhaps for as little as possessing a different color skin).

When a visitor comes to the bridge at night, turns their headlights off for a minute, then turns them back on, they can reportedly see the shadowy image of a man hanging from the bridge structure. The shadow dissolves over the next few seconds and then it looks as if there was never

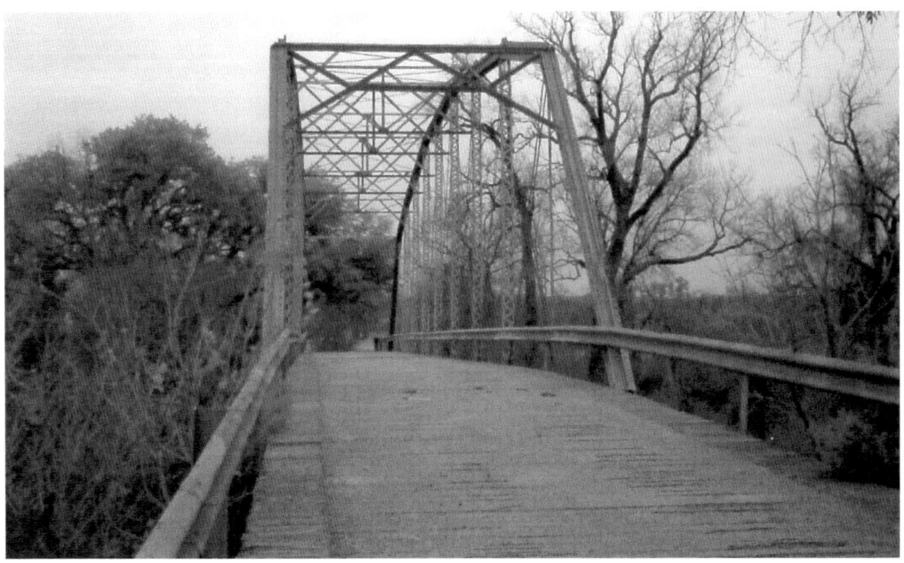

Original Maxdale Bridge crossing the Lampasas River.

anything there but the old broken down remnants of a bridge that is no longer used.

A witch coven was reported to meet below the span in the early 1900s. They supposedly built bonfires and danced naked in the moonlight while performing their sacred rituals.

Tales are told of orb-like lights that have been seen moving around on the bridge late at night. Other stories are told of eerie lights that appeared and moved about in the middle of the deserted cemetery. Could these lights be ghost hunters' flashlights, lanterns or cameras? Could the lights be the manifestation of the spirits of the dearly departed returning to roam the earth? Could the lights that are seen be some sort of swamp gas or Saint Elmo's fire? Could the lights be spiritual sparks from the old witch bonfires that were built below the bridge's span? Or maybe it was just the drink-addled imagination of inebriated locals?

One story tells of a vehicle being left in neutral that began eerily moving slowly away from the bridge with no one inside. It was on the south side of the bridge, and the vehicle slowly picked up speed and ended almost at the gate to the Maxdale Cemetery. As there was a slight incline leading up to the entrance of the bridge, not putting a vehicle in park was probably a really bad decision on the part of the owner but still made for a whopper of a tale.

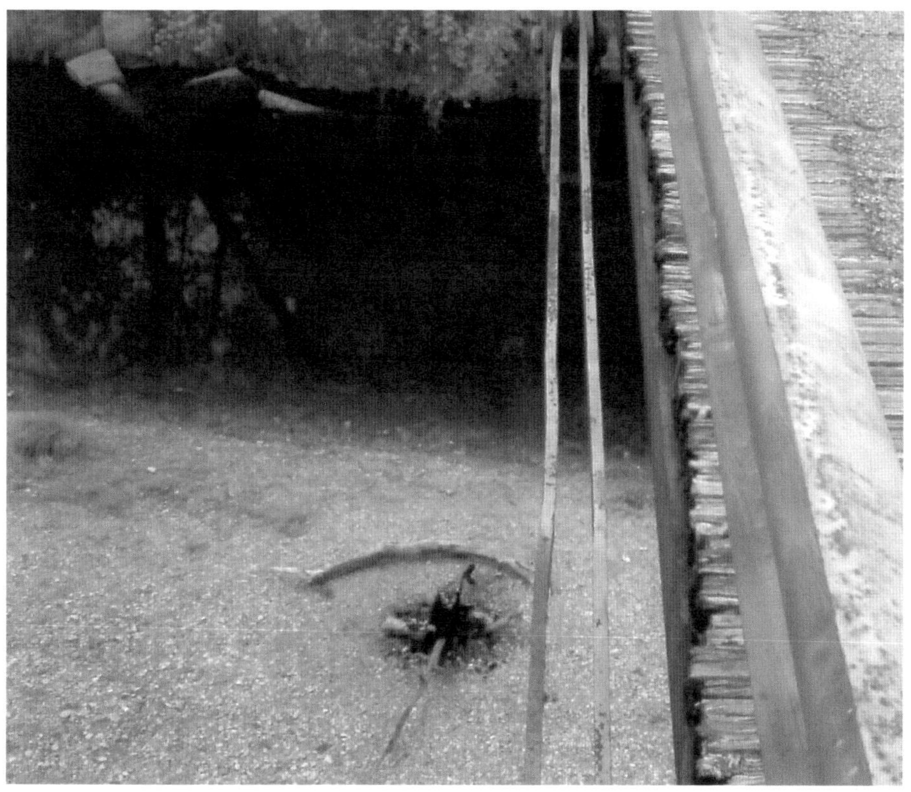

Remains of a bonfire below the Maxdale Bridge. Do Wiccan practitioners still meet here?

But that was not the only tale told of vehicles being moved by ghostly means on and around the bridge.

Flooding due to storms is not uncommon in the area. One 2007 flood in Killeen was large enough to jerk mobile homes free of their tie-downs and hurl them downstream, smashing into bridge abutments.

It was during one of the worst of these storms in the mid-1900s that flooding threatened to wash away the Maxdale Bridge. The water rose up above the entrances on both ends of the bridge and almost reached the bottom. The Maxdale Cemetery groundskeeper raced over to the bridge to try to flag down vehicles to prevent them from crossing and perhaps being washed away by the raging floodwaters.

His attempt was for naught. The first vehicle to approach was occupied by an inebriated local couple. The driver had just proposed, and she had accepted. They had been celebrating their engagement with a bit too much

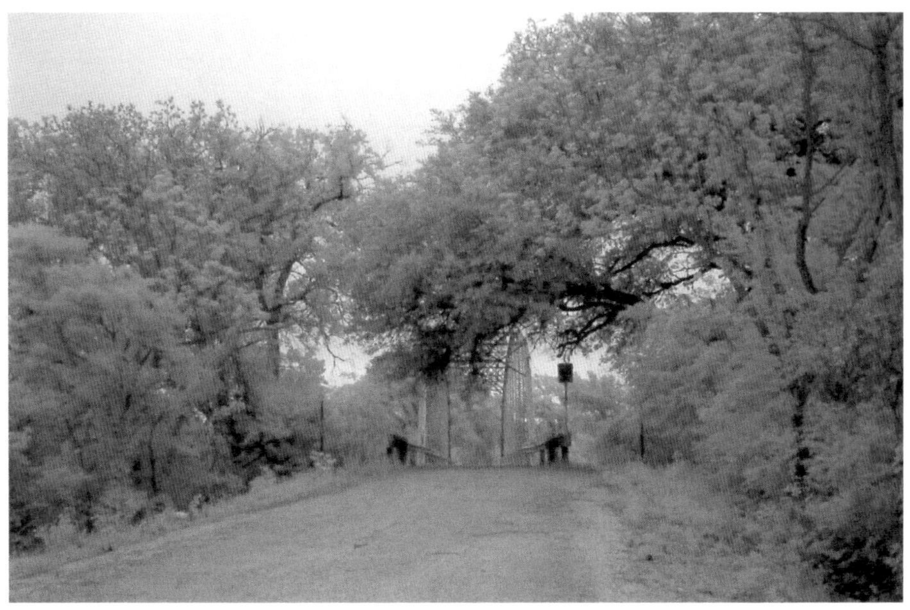

A shadow appears to be hanging over the rail, gazing into the river below.

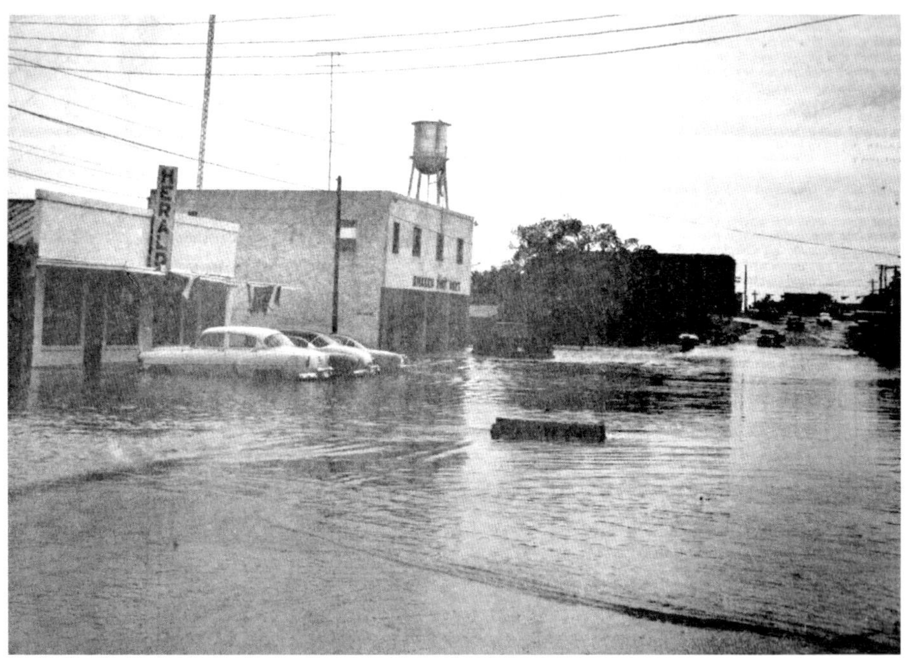

Flooding in Killeen.

alcohol. The groundskeeper attempted to flag them down, but the driver's limited concentration was on his bride-to-be. Seeing the groundskeeper at the last moment he swerved to avoid him—right into the path of an oncoming school bus. Swerving farther to avoid the school bus, the car raced off the side of the bridge into the raging torrent of water below. At that same moment, the bus driver swerved to avoid the car and struck the groundskeeper and the side of the bridge.

The groundskeeper was instantly killed, but the bus only went halfway off the bridge, teetering slowly back and forth. A gust of wind-driven rain completed the task, and the bus with the screaming children plunged into the deadly floodwaters. None of the children or the bus driver survived.

The driver of the first vehicle managed to escape his car and was found clinging to a tree limb the next day. His fiancée's body was never recovered. Despondent over his loss, blaming himself and wanting to be forever with his lost lover, he hanged himself below the bridge. His body was discovered by coven members who had gathered to celebrate their pagan rituals.

There have been reports of visitors hearing children screaming softly in the distance. The sound of squealing tires and the crunch of metal striking metal from the side of the bridge have also been heard.

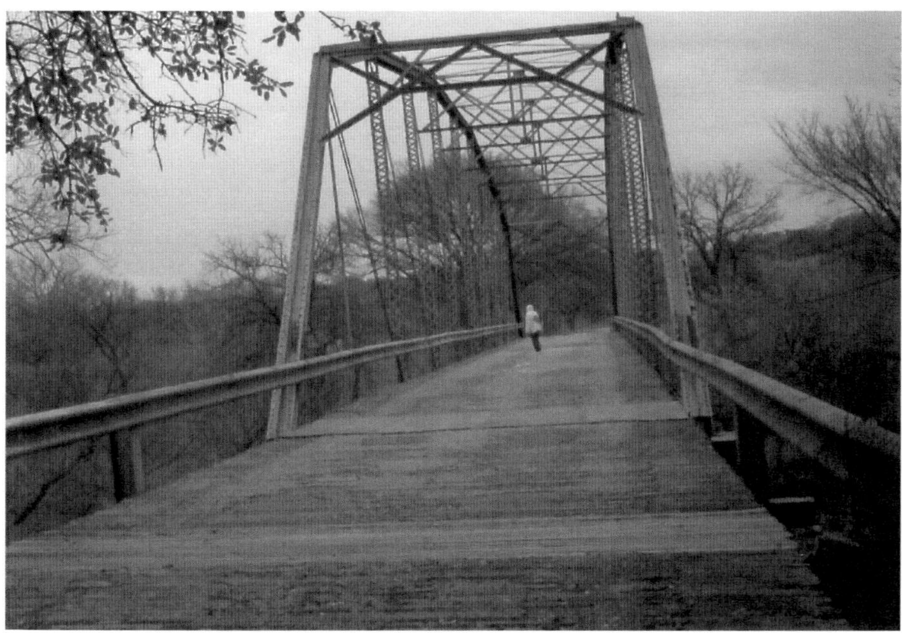

An investigator sees what appears to be a winged apparition at the end of the Maxdale Bridge.

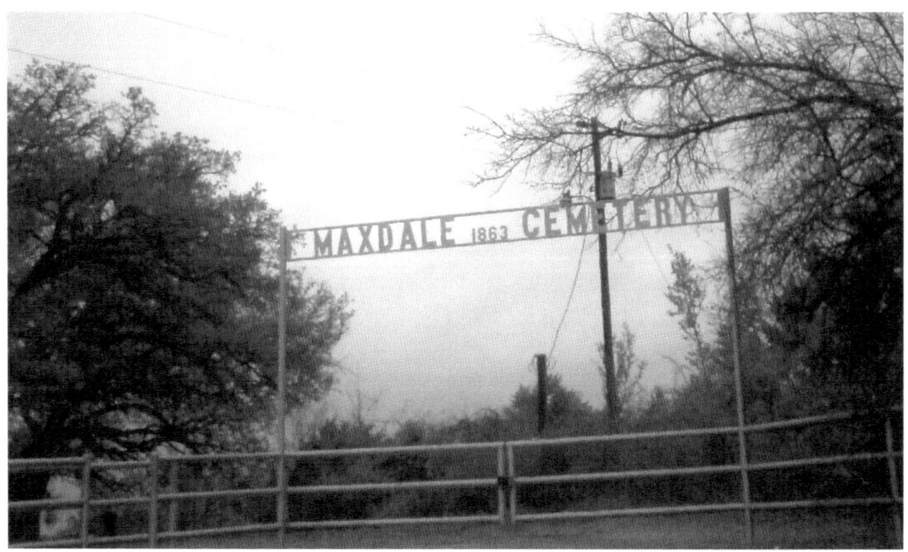

Entrance to Maxdale Cemetery.

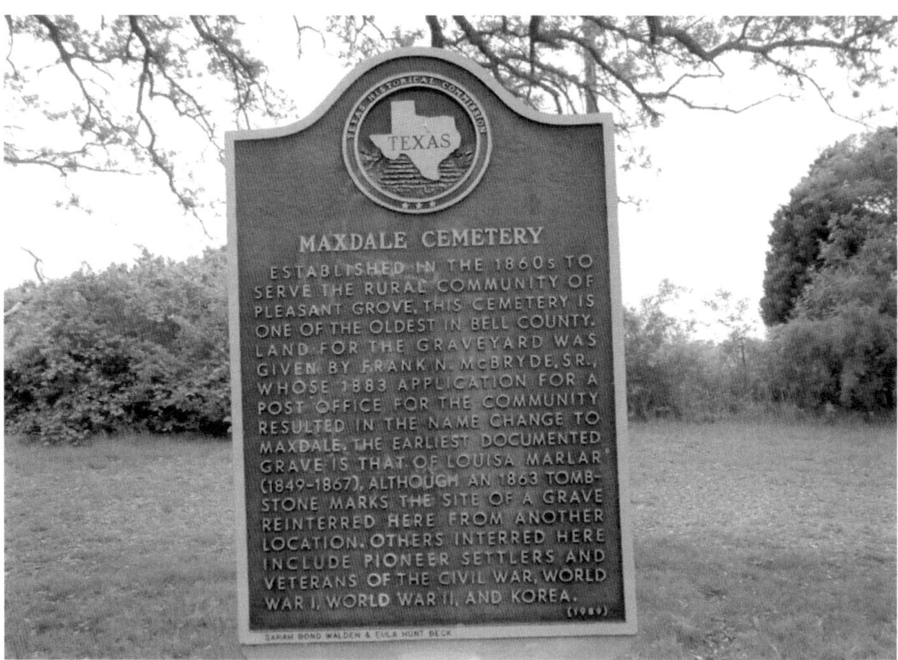

Maxdale Cemetery monument.

It has also been reported that if visitors go on the bridge during a full moon, they can see shadowy images of the children floating in the water.

People have reported finding small fingerprints in the dirt of their cars, as if there were children trying to push the car away from the bridge to keep it safe from the water's fury.

Some visitors to the cemetery have reported that they had been met by a nice elderly gentleman in the cemetery. He claimed to be the caretaker and was always very helpful and assisted the visitors in finding a specific gravestone or a loved one who made their final resting place here.

Once they have been directed to the right spot, they turn to thank him… and he is gone. They look around the cemetery, and he is nowhere to be found. Was he the ghost of the old caretaker, the one who died in the flood? Or was he just a helpful local hunter who was really good at camouflage?

15

Triple Seven Sighting

Just south of Killeen, near the area locally known as Triple Seven, lived a family of hardworking people. They used to like to sit on the porch and gaze at the peacefulness of the surrounding trees and fields. While they believed in spirits and the afterlife, they had never actually seen anything to validate those beliefs.

The beloved brother passed away early in the morning in January a couple of years ago. His sister, heartbroken, later brought a camera out and took pictures of the view that they had both enjoyed in an attempt to keep his memory alive within her.

When she looked back at the pictures a few months later, she was astonished. There was something that had not been there when she took the photographs—something strange that had not been visible to her naked eyes. But what was it? What did she find in the photos that had not been there before?

It looked like an orb, slowly floating away from the property. Was it the spirit of her deceased brother, visiting the backyard for the last time? That is what she believed.

When out in the Triple Seven area, look to the skies and watch for his spirit floating above you, revisiting the land that he loved. You never know what you may find watching you back.

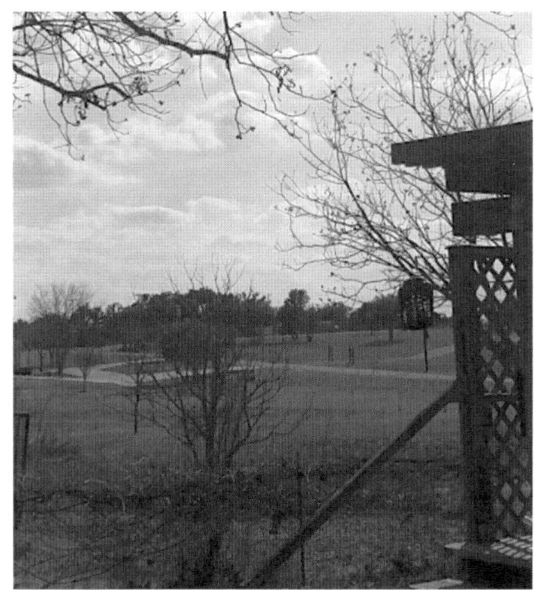

Right: Backyard in Triple Seven, south of Killeen.

Below: An orb floating behind a tree.

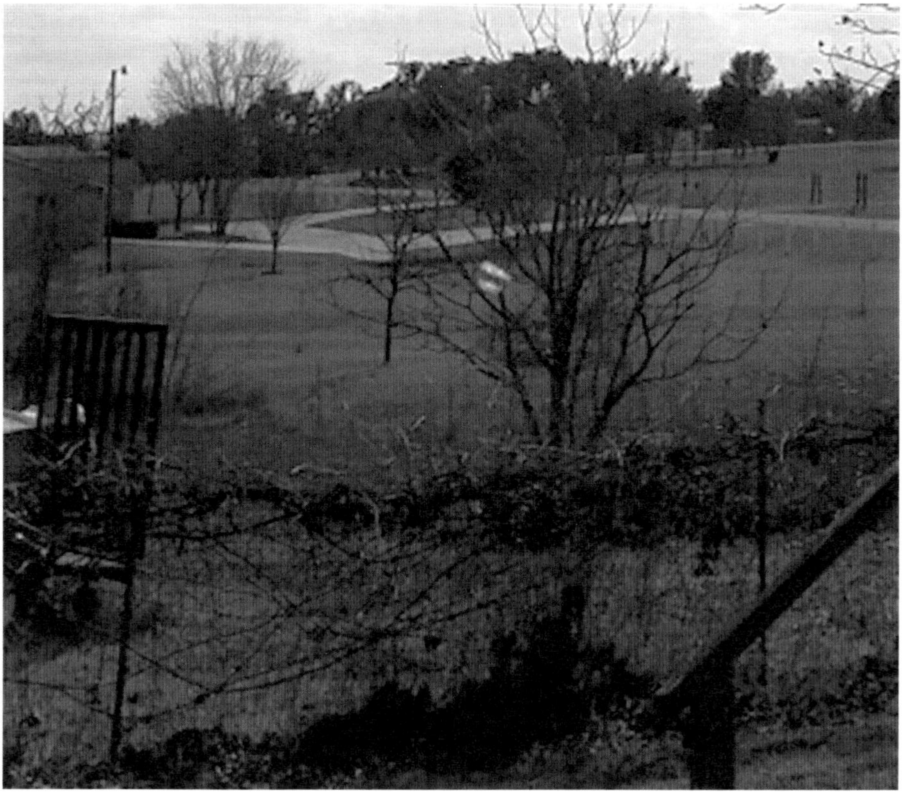

16

Fort Hood Phantom

Fort Hood, founded in 1942 as Camp Hood, is one of the largest military bases in the world both in size and population. It was named after Confederate general John Bell Hood. Fort Hood was sited to sit at the intersection of three counties: Bell, Coryell and Lampasas. Small communities were involuntarily relocated to allow for the construction of the base.

Unfortunately, no effort was made to let the spirits of the deceased former residents know. It is thought that they still roam the countryside at night, seeking their former homes. Some of them may have decided to occupy military housing units to make up for the lack of their former residences, those involuntarily moved to make way for the military might.

One such story comes from a young couple with a three-year-old daughter. They arrived at Fort Hood and were given a military housing duplex when the husband, a junior soldier, was assigned to the base. They had just had the furniture set up and a few boxes unpacked when they had to settle down for their first night in their new residence.

Starting the first night, the wife felt there was something wrong, like it wasn't really their home, but someone else's. Her first night was a restless one, with her waking repeatedly with feelings of dread.

The first few weeks went by slowly, and the feelings persisted. Having unpacked most of the boxes with the family's personal items seemed to make the home feel better, but it still did not feel like it was hers.

One restless night, when her husband was away on duty, she awoke in horror, hearing her daughter's terrified screams coming from her room. Racing out of her bedroom and down the hall, she tore into her daughter's room to find her little girl hiding under her covers screaming "No, No, No!" at the top of her lungs. She threw herself onto the bed and pulled her daughter out from the covers and into her arms, hugging her tightly to her chest.

Rocking her crying daughter back and forth, she tried soothing her to calm her down. The daughter was shaking uncontrollably, and her screaming changed to sobbing into her mother's shoulder. When she finally got her daughter calmed down a bit, all she could get her to say was, "It's here."

With her daughter in her arms, the mother got up and checked around the room. Nothing seemed wrong—some toys were scattered about on the floor, but that was normal for her daughter. It was a difficult task to teach a three-year-old to put away her toys at night. Thinking perhaps the little girl was afraid of monsters in her room, the mother turned on the light and showed her daughter there was nothing in the closet or under the bed.

As she pulled the covers back to put her daughter back in the bed, she noticed a small child-sized dirty handprint on the edge of the bottom

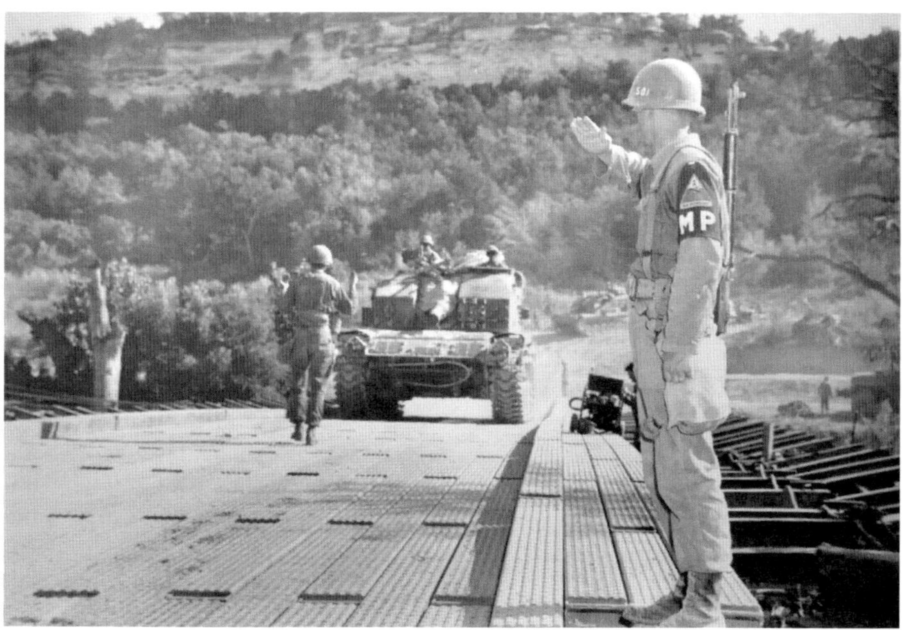

Fort Hood, Texas.

sheet. She had given her daughter a bath before tucking her into bed but checked her hands anyway just in case she had gotten them dirty again. They were spotless.

Frowning to herself, thinking her daughter made the print after playing in the yard, she made a mental note to change the sheet. She suddenly realized something was strange about the print and turned back to examine it closer. Comparing it to her daughter's diminutive hand, she realized it was a little larger—not quite as large as an adult's, but still bigger than what her daughter should have left.

Her daughter started sobbing again and reaching out for her, so she lay down beside her daughter and held her for comfort. They fell asleep together.

The next morning, she laundered all of the sheets and warned her daughter about washing her hands if she played outside. Her daughter seemed unfazed by the previous night's problems. Perhaps it was just some kind of night terrors that children were prone to and would grow out of.

Later that day, she noticed her daughter sitting on the floor of her room talking to herself. When she asked her daughter if she was alright, her daughter told her she was talking with her friend. Knowing children occasionally have imaginary friends, she asked what her new friend looked like. Her daughter scrunched up her face with her hands and growled.

Thinking that her daughter had either an ugly dog or child as a friend, she bent down to give her daughter a kiss on the cheek and froze. Her daughter's dress had two dirty handprints on it. Even knowing her daughter hadn't been outside, she looked at her hands anyway. Her hands were clean. The prints were a little larger than her daughter's, about the same size as the handprint on the sheet. Quickly picking up her daughter, she brought her downstairs.

Not knowing what else to do, she grabbed her keys, ran out to her car and raced to the medical clinic. The physician's assistant checked out her daughter but found nothing physically wrong. After eliciting the full story from the mother, he recommended she make an appointment for her daughter with a pediatric psychiatrist. He also recommended she make an appointment for herself.

Disgusted with the implication she was seeing things, she went back to her house. She sat in the car for a while staring at her side of the duplex. Finally making up her mind that nothing was going to drive her out, she took her child out of her car seat and resolutely walked up to the door. Pausing only momentarily to unlock the door, she stormed into the house. Everything looked normal.

When her husband got home, she sat him down on the sofa and told him what had happened. He just smiled in an irritating way and claimed that any new house had quirks that took a little getting used to. Indignant, she almost slapped him but, instead, stood up and stomped off to the kitchen.

After dinner, they sat watching television in the cramped living room. Junior military housing tended to be fairly compact, and this one was no different. Her husband suddenly sat up and looked back at the stairs with a strange look on his face. Shaking his head, he turned back to the television. She asked what it was, and he told her he heard soft footsteps on the stairs behind him. Both of them could see their daughter was sitting in the corner playing with a doll.

The wife looked back at the stairs with trepidation but heard nothing. With chills running down her back, she snuggled closer to her husband. Her husband suddenly jumped out of the chair and turned toward the back of the couch. He asked her if she heard anything.

When she denied hearing anything, he told her he heard a small voice behind him say "Hi." The couch was pushed up against the wall. They looked behind the couch, but there was nothing there. He shook his head in disbelief, carefully bent over beside the couch and looked behind it. There was nothing between the couch and the wall.

He suddenly realized the wall behind the sofa was a shared wall with the living room in the other half of the duplex right behind it. Chuckling, he took a seat and explained to his wife he must have heard something from the family on the other side. She looked apprehensively at the wall then sat down beside him again.

Her daughter suddenly looked up, dropped her doll and clapped her hands joyfully. She stood up and ran to sit beside the couch. She began to talk quietly and then shushed whatever she was talking to. The husband looked at his daughter strangely until his wife explained that it must be her new imaginary friend. Still not sure what to make of the situation, he turned back to the television.

Later, his wife took their daughter upstairs, gave her a bath and put her to bed. She came back down and sat back down on the couch.

After an hour, the husband got a quizzical look on his face and glanced back at the stairs. He asked his wife if she had put their child in bed. When she told him she had, he stood up, went to the bottom of the stairs and looked up. Coming back to the couch, he told her he could have sworn he saw his daughter on the stairs or at least the shadow of her legs. His wife got up and went upstairs to check but found her daughter fast asleep in bed.

She came back down and asked if he was trying to scare her. He laughed and said he was tired and must have been seeing things. They turned off the television and went to bed.

The next Sunday, they went to church. After services, she spoke with the chaplain and explained what was going on. He smiled indulgently and asked if she would like him to bless her house. She smiled with relief and said that was exactly what she wanted. They arranged for him to come over the next day and conduct the blessing.

Later that day, after preparing supper for her family, she heard her daughter up in her room playing with her friend again. She called up to the girl to come down and eat, but her daughter ignored her. Unhappy that her daughter preferred an imaginary friend to a healthy meal, she went upstairs to her daughter's room.

Beside her daughter's bed she saw her daughter sitting on the floor facing what appeared to be another child. The child had on dirty, torn-up rags that might at one time have been an old-fashioned gingham dress. Her dirty, bedraggled hair hung down her back. Frightened, the woman called to her daughter again. Both children turned to look at her.

She froze in horror as she gazed on the other child's face. Most of the face was bare, dirty skull with shreds of skin hanging off. It looked like the creature was trying to force its decomposing face into a smile for her. Her daughter got up and came across the room to where her mother stood petrified in the doorway.

Fear freezing her voice and unable to do anything else, she grabbed her daughter's hand, swept her out of the room and tore down the stairs taking them three at a time. She ran to the front door, tore it open and raced out of the house in panic.

As she stood in the street looking back at the house, her husband came out and asked her what was wrong. She started babbling, as she couldn't articulate what she had seen. Her husband took her in his arms and asked if she wanted to go back into the house with him.

Shaking her head violently, he led her over to the car and locked her inside. He went back through the still-open front door and went upstairs. After a while he came back down, closed the front door of the house and climbed into the car with her. He told her he didn't see anything upstairs and again asked what it was she saw.

She finally managed to gasp out her tale of the decomposed young girl she had seen their daughter playing with. Her husband gave the house a strange look and asked if she would feel better if they spent the night in a hotel. Relieved, she quickly agreed, and they went to the Poxon Guest House on base. The Poxon was a small hotel on Fort Hood used exclusively by military families and retirees visiting the area.

While there, the wife accessed the internet and searched for local paranormal groups. Finding one, she called and tried to explain what had happened to the woman who answered the phone. They recommended the house be blessed and then purged of residual spirits. Telling her she had already arranged for a blessing, she asked how she could get the house purged. The woman on the phone got her information and said she would try to arrange to come out the following day after the priest completed his task there. Relieved, the wife enjoyed her first full night's rest in a long time.

The following day, her husband went to work, and she dropped her daughter off to a daycare on base. She spent part of the day at the post exchange, then, at the proper time, went to the house to let the priest in. He walked about with a Bible and holy water and blessed the house and all within it. She stayed outside and thanked him when he was done.

Shortly after he left, a woman and man drove up and parked in front of their house. They must be the ones from the paranormal group. She had been expecting them to be driving some weird vehicle with lights and sirens like something out of an old movie, but no, it was just a plain small Ford Focus with no indication of the occupants' unusual vocation. They got out and introduced themselves, and the frightened woman explained the priest had just left after his blessing.

They got a small case out of the car, and she let them in the house. She wasn't about to go back in until everything was done. The couple went in and walked throughout the residence. They then opened all of the windows and doors in the house. They lit sage branches and walked about while saying something. She was too far away to hear what they were saying but wasn't about to get any closer till they were done.

The couple extinguished the sage, closed the doors and windows and went back out to talk with her. The woman said she was a sensitive, and there did appear to have been a presence in the house. She said she didn't believe it was malevolent or hostile to their presence; it was just a residual spirit, perhaps left over from when the base moved all of the civilians off the land to make way for the installation. They may have left unidentified graves, and this might have been the deceased child of one of those farmers or ranchers. They explained that the spirit was gone, and she should have no more experiences.

Thankful, she paid them and went to get her daughter out of daycare. The family returned to the house and have had no problem since.

Did the spirit move on into the afterlife, eventually finding peace? Or did it just move on to another residence in the housing area? Only time and other residents will tell.

17
Hood Housing Horror

Another story of terror comes from another, more recent, resident of housing on base. Once the young couple and their one-year-old son moved into their new home, they began to have feelings of being watched. The wife reported the watcher seemed to be an unseen male and she routinely felt his presence when she was in the bathroom. The presence disturbed her, but she passed it off as just her imagination.

Then she noticed irregular activity of her young son. Just barely able to crawl, he would move over to the stairs and stare at one specific spot. She checked it out to see if maybe a bug was there and he was watching it, but no, it was just the wall. He began doing this more and more. Then, in the evenings, he began to simply stare at a specific spot on the ceiling in her room. Worried, she took him in to the medical clinic, but he was given a clean bill of health.

At night. she heard the sound of boots stomping around but assumed it was just coming from the other side of the duplex. Military housing was known for having paper-thin walls, and noisy neighbors were a given in the military.

Shortly after that, while her husband was away on duty, she lay on the couch watching television. She suddenly heard footsteps stomping up beside her. Sitting up quickly, she looked around, expecting to see her husband surprising her by coming home early. There was no one there. She looked back at the television to see if maybe it was something there, but the characters were sitting on a couch talking, not walking. Besides, it had sounded as if it was right beside her, beside the couch, not toward the television, and the sound was down low as her baby was sleeping upstairs.

Maybe the sound came from the neighbors, since the walls were so thin in the duplex, but no, they were away on vacation. The sound of footsteps couldn't have come from next door.

Being a brave military wife, she went in the kitchen and pulled out a long knife. She slowly moved about the house searching for the source of the noise. No one was there. She found her baby awake and staring at the same point on the ceiling. Not knowing what to do, she sat on her bed and guarded her child until she fell asleep on the bed.

The next morning, she found the television downstairs was off. She didn't remember turning it off when she went upstairs. Again, she got the feeling someone was watching her.

Several days later, while her husband was still away for training, she was relaxing upstairs with her child. The house was quiet, but suddenly she began to hear a whispering. It sounded like it was coming from the stairwell. With a shiver going down her spine and goose bumps on her arms, she slowly rose and moved toward the door to the hall. The whispering got louder and was joined by the distant sound of rushing water. Sticking her head slowly into the hallway, she found the noise appeared to be coming from the direction of the stairwell.

She pressed her back against the wall and slid herself along the wall down the hallway toward the stairwell. She peeked around the corner but saw nothing that would be causing the noise. Moving out onto the landing, she noticed the noise appeared to be coming from the exact spot her son had been staring at for the last several months.

She started down the stairs toward the noise when she felt something shove her backward. She fell back on the stairs and pushed herself up several steps toward the landing. Looking around with fright, she noticed a toy sitting on the step she had been about to put her foot on. If she had taken one more step, she could have slipped on the toy and been severely injured falling down the rest of the stairs.

Shaking from her close call, and halfway convinced whatever shoved her meant her no harm, she retreated back up into her bedroom and closed the door, muffling the sounds still resonating in the hall. She took her son from his crib and hugged him to her the rest of the night.

When her husband returned she begged him to have them move out. She explained what happened, but he didn't seem to truly believe her tale. Reluctantly, he found a house available in nearby Killeen and moved there. The entity apparently did not follow them to their new abode. Yet.

18
WHAT ARE GHOSTS?

Ghosts exist. Ghosts are sometimes called by different names, such as spirits, apparitions, entities, imps, phantasms, orbs, poltergeists, shadows, shades, sprites, fairies, angels, devils, elementals, djinn and demons. While ghosts may be called by a variety of different names and while each of the entities may display different types of physical, audible and olfactory manifestations, the actual physical existence of paranormal spirits is generally believed in by a large percentage of the world's population. The very term *paranormal* has been defined as meaning "beyond the normal" or, more simply put, something that science is unable to rationally explain at this time.

Though many people may deny it, the vast majority of the population of the world has either seen, heard, touched, smelled, sensed or been touched by something that they could not readily identify or explain. Quite often, those who were involved have decided that what occurred or what they observed could not have been naturally occurring or been caused by anything earthly and that it had to have been caused by some sort of paranormal ghosts or spirits.

Ghosts and hauntings have even been introduced to our court system. A seller tried to sell a house reported to be possessed by spirits in New York. In 1991, a state court of appeals in New York ruled that the house was haunted as a matter of law and did not require a determination of the facts by a jury.[5]

This decision is significant because when something is ruled a matter of law, it becomes an undeniable truth, a fact that the lawyers and lower courts would be unable to dispute. This ruling could even serve as a reasonable precedent for other courts in other states to rule that buildings and locations were the home for haunts. The full ruling by the court that the residence was legally determined to have been haunted can be found in *Stambovsky v. Ackley* in the New York Court of Appeals. The Stambovsky ruling also determined that the residence could not be turned over unoccupied or vacant to the buyer because the resident spirits still resided there.[6]

Just because the conservative justices of a state court of appeals ruled that ghosts exist does not necessarily mean that everything that goes bump in the night is caused by a ghost.

Most unusual occurrences have been found to have a reasonable and rational scientific explanation. This simple fact may not be easily discernable to those who have just been frightened out of their wits. It has been found that in the absence of an immediately discernable reasonable, rational or natural scientific explanation, an unusual or abnormal occurrence has quite often been classified as beyond the normal or paranormal. Another term that has been used by people to describe something beyond what they are comfortable with is *supernatural*. Supernatural and paranormal have frequently been used interchangeably by researchers. It is the understandable fear of being ridiculed or called a hoaxer for saying they saw or heard something paranormal that would make people feel uncomfortable about reporting these unusual experiences or even talking about them to friends.

As most people agree that ghosts exist, the next question that most people want answered is to find out what ghosts are made up of. It is well known that the universe is filled with different types of energy. Even matter has been found to be made up of energy when it is viewed in its purest form of subatomic particles. The concept that energy cannot be created or destroyed and can only be changed from one form to another has become known as the law of conservation of energy and is considered to be the first law of thermodynamics, a basic law of science.

In a 2014 *Scientific American* article, Clara Moskowitz reported that this law of thermodynamics provides the basis for a theory that says the energy in a closed system will remain constant unless it is acted upon by an outside influence.[7] Quite a few prominent paranormal researchers have theorized that ghosts or paranormal entities are simply the continued physical manifestation of the energy that was originally contained within humans or animals that have passed away. This belief is consistent with the first law of thermodynamics in that the contained energy does not simply vanish, it merely changes state.

Victor Zamit has postulated there are seven laws of psychic energy.[8] The laws of paranormal forces parallel the laws of psychic energy in many ways, but they do not fully explain the paranormal. Thus, there are seven laws of paranormal forces that are intended to attempt to explain paranormal or supernatural activity and the spirit world. They are as follows:

First Law of Paranormal Forces

Paranormal energy is neither created nor destroyed; it is only transformed from one state to another.

This paranormal force law is almost identical to the first law of thermodynamics. A paranormal entity utilizes energy to cause physical manifestations and to materialize and dematerialize itself. This utilization by the paranormal entity is not creating or destroying energy, it is the transformation of energy and thus is in keeping with the laws of thermodynamics.

Second Law of Paranormal Forces

Everything physical is made up of vibrational energy.

The concept that all physical objects are made up of some sort of vibrational energy is consistent with the bulk of scientific research that has discovered that all physical matter is made up of packets of energy when it is viewed in its purest form of subatomic particles. Changing the speed of these particles can change their state of matter, similar to how water will turn to ice when the vibrational energy is slowed sufficiently (cooled) and will turn to steam when the vibrational energy is increased sufficiently (heated).

Third Law of Paranormal Forces

Paranormal entities operate at vibrational frequencies and light spectrums that are typically not visible to the human eye.

The vibrational energy of matter is characterized by its temperature. Higher vibrational energy states have proportionally higher temperatures.

Gasses that are invisible to the human eye can become visible when they are cooled and change state to become either liquid or solid. Similarly, when a solid or a liquid is heated up, it can vaporize and possibly no longer be visible to the unaided human eye. This materialization and dematerialization is a commonly occurring reasonable and rational scientific process.

Another example of this concept is light waves. The vibration or frequency of light determines its wavelength. Human eyes are limited and are only able to observe a very narrow band or frequency of light waves. The higher speed or frequency light waves tend to be invisible to the human eye. The paranormal entity would have to alter its energy level to physically manifest itself to humans. When the frequency of these light waves is slowed, they can become detectable by humans and may be seen to materialize.

If the paranormal entities are operating at high wavelengths, frequencies or vibrational energy states, they may well be imperceptible to the normal unenhanced human senses; this could explain why so few entities have actually been observed or recorded.

When the vibrational speed of entities is slowed, they become visible. When the vibrational speed of entities is accelerated, they vanish. Ectoplasmic energy that is expended by the entities in the deceleration or acceleration of their vibrational energy state can be physically detected. This transformational usage or energy shows up as a detectable amount of electromagnetic energy given off during the change in state.

FOURTH LAW OF PARANORMAL FORCES

Plants, animals and humans are all made up of different levels and types of vibrational energy.

Material creatures are made up of different levels and types of vibrational energy. This concept is exemplified when the creature passes away. A portion of the pre-existing vibrational energy remains with the physical material body but the vibrational energy that makes up the spirit or essence of the creature continues on at a higher vibrational energy and it is no longer restrained by the physical containment of the physical body. This higher vibrational energy level is very difficult for humans to discern without mechanical or electronic assistance though some people have claimed to "see" it. As with the first and second laws, the idea that the material physical body is made up of different types of vibrational energy is consistent with the first law of thermodynamics in that it postulates that energy is neither created nor destroyed, the existing energy merely changes state.

FIFTH LAW OF PARANORMAL FORCES

The vibrational energy contained within living plants, animals and humans that are the essence of souls is detectable.

There are some individuals who are reportedly able to detect wavelengths and energy fields that are not normally visible to the human eye. These individuals are supposed to be able to observe the energy field that surrounds individuals, animals and objects. The energy field is known as the human energy field or, more commonly, the aura.

The color of the aura is reportedly representative of the nature and personality of the individual, nice and kind, nasty and evil or much more commonly, somewhere in between the extremes. It is believed that the more spiritually evolved individuals are, the kinder and gentler they would be, which would mean they would tend to have a lighter aura. This type of aura would appear brighter and would give off more energy. The less spiritually evolved would be an individual tending to be more prone to evil, and they would have a much darker or black aura. This type of aura would tend to suck in the energy from around it.

It is also believed that the aura may represent an energy field that could possibly be able to control external physical objects and events. This concept may provide the basis behind the scientific experimentation that has been conducted in telepathy, telekinetic, teleportation, out-of-body experiences and the seemingly supernatural bond that has been found to link some twins.

Sixth Law of Paranormal Forces

Vibrational energy, auras or a portion thereof can be imprinted from humans onto objects or locations.

Extreme emotion can cause a portion of an entity's vibrational energy to become trapped or contained in an object or location. An example of this is the ocean just off of the Cape of Good Hope. A large number of ships have been damaged or destroyed in storms at this location. The sheer terror of the passengers and crews who died in that area has imprinted on the location. A ghostly ship has been repeatedly sighted at or near this location over the centuries, appearing as a sailing ship with people on deck desperately trying to contact the ship sighting them. Slowly the sailing ship dissipates into the mist and ocean spray. This famous imprinting has become widely known as the legend of the Flying Dutchman.

Seventh Law of Paranormal Forces

There are vibrational energy fields that were never plant, animal or human.

There exist some entities that seemingly were never earthly beings. This would include certain uncommon types of manifestations, such as imps, demons, devils, djinn and angels, which were believed to have never been living humans or animals and were never possessed of any creature's energy per religious dogma.

On the other hand, it is possible that angels are just entities that were really, really good people in their previous life and all of the other entities could just be the psychic remains of the practical jokers, psychologically impaired, evil minded or deranged humans who have died.

Paranormal researchers have found that not all hauntings or the physical manifestations of paranormal entities are alike, and there tends to be a wide variety of possible identifiable and observable paranormal activity. Some of the unexplained events may present a single type of physical manifestation and may possibly repeat the same occurrence over and over again. Other hauntings may exhibit several different types of activities that do not on the surface appear to have any possible rational or reasonable scientific explanation. Examples of these unidentifiable occurrences include but are not limited to the following:

- An unexpected or unidentifiable noise is heard.
- An apparent motion seen only in the corner of the eye.
- Footsteps heard when no one else is around.
- A door or window that opens or closes without human intervention
- A light or shadow where none should be.
- Items found in different locations than where they were left.
- Unusual unexplainable odors, such as perfume, smoke, sulfur and so forth.
- Lights turning off and on without human intervention.
- Areas that seem to be abnormally hot or cold without the heat or air being on.
- The hairs on the back of the neck rising.
- Pets start acting differently than normal.
- A feeling of dread coming over someone with no apparent cause.
- Disembodied voices or electronic voice phenomena (EVP).
- Physical contact when no one else is around.
- The sudden appearance of an apparition.
- A physical attack on an occupant or investigator

Any of these manifestations could be caused by paranormal activity, but there could also be a rational scientific explanation for whatever is believed to have been observed. Each of these different types of manifestations will be covered later separately and discussed in depth.

As mentioned before, there are a wide variety of names for ghosts. The simple reason for this is the vast amount of differences in the physical manifestations exhibited by the different types and kinds of entities.

19
Types of Ghosts

Angels

Angels are considered by religious individuals to be positive energy entities that are in the service of and doing the bidding of God. These paranormal entities are typically believed in by a wide variety of religious practitioners, and in most cases, they are considered to represent the theological concept of good. Angels are considered by most occupants and investigators to be nonthreatening and represent no cause for concern.

Apparition

An apparition is the unexplained sudden physical appearance of what seems to be a deceased person or animal or a portion thereof. These apparitions are typically dark, translucent and materialize as a shadow, a full body apparition or, more commonly, as a smaller portion of a human or animal body. Apparitions have been found to be nonthreatening entities but may be disconcerting to the observer.

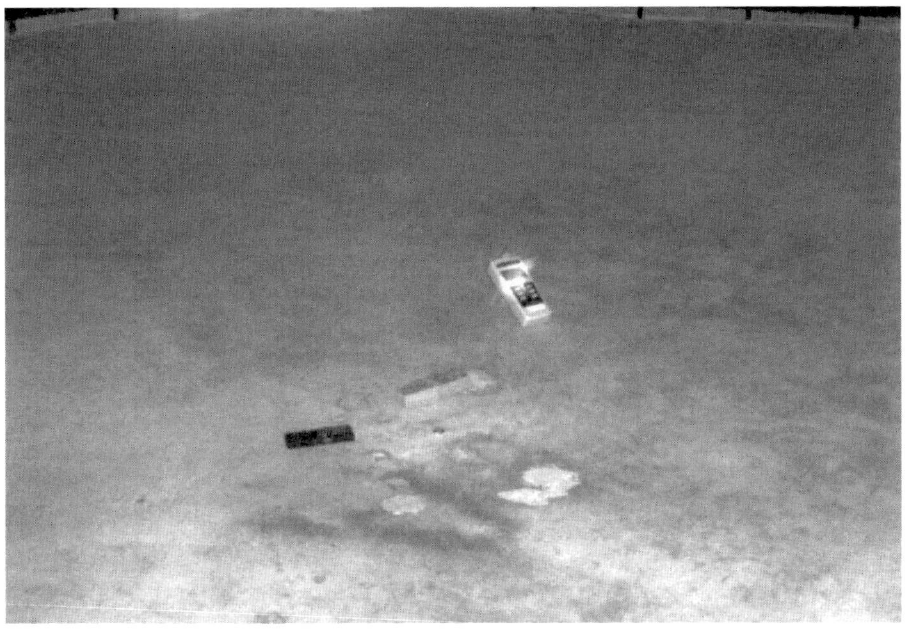

Disembodied hand grabbing at a Mel Meter?

DEMON

Demons have been found by researchers to be extremely malevolent spirits that are almost always actively aggressive and antagonistic toward occupants and investigators. If there has been major damage done to personal property or to a building, violent physical attacks against occupants or investigators or the violent possession of a human occupant or investigator, it is probably indicative of the presence of a demon. Demons are entities that are better left to the careful ministrations of exorcists from a religious organization or to a professional demonologist and should be avoided by occupants, researchers and investigators if at all possible.

DEVIL

Devils are considered by religious individuals to be extremely negative energy entities. The term *devil* is sometimes used in literature interchangeably with *demon*. These extremely malevolent spirits are typically believed in by a variety of religious individuals and are usually considered to represent the theological concept of evil. Most religious leaders have preached that devils were originally angels fallen from the grace of God (a.k.a. fallen angels). Devils are entities that are better left to the careful ministrations of exorcists from a religious organization or a professional demonologist and should be avoided by occupants, researchers and investigators if at all possible.

DJINN

A djinn is an Islamic version of an imp but just a little more dangerous. Djinn would almost seem to be equivalent to a lessor form of a demon. Djinn are reported to act in ways similar to imps, taking objects, moving items around, starting fires and generally harassing people. They also are reportedly able to take possession of people just like demons. While these entities appear to be less dangerous than demons, they would still require the use of religious exorcists or a professional demonologist to exorcise them and should be avoided by occupants, researchers and investigators if at all possible.

ECTOPLASM

Ectoplasm is believed to be the material substance that entities are made up of. Residual ectoplasm is not usually found in large quantities and can be observed as a mist or as a trace substance that is sometimes left behind on materials by certain types of manifestations. Residual ectoplasm will either rapidly evaporate or be quickly absorbed by the material it was deposited on upon the departure of an observed entity. Ectoplasm may occasionally erroneously be referred to by investigators as mist, although mist may well be made up of ectoplasm.

Elemental

An elemental is a paranormal entity that is sometimes believed to be just another name for a demon. While there may be a wide variety of elementals having a wide variety of different reported abilities, the same can be said of demons. They are reportedly entities of negative ectoplasmic energy that have a hostile attitude toward humans and our plane of existence.

Elementals are believed to have been brought forth into our world by the practitioners of black magic who hoped to exert control over them and have the elementals do their bidding. Regretfully, some of the conjured elementals may have been stronger than the practitioner of the magic anticipated and whatever protective spells they may have tried to use may have been insufficient to contain the conjured entity.

Elementals are entities that are better left to the careful ministrations of exorcists from a religious organization or to a professional demonologist and should be avoided by occupants, researchers and investigators if at all possible.

Entity

The term *entity* is a generic name used by paranormal investigators to refer to all forms of paranormal creatures that are identified as having caused a manifestation, but the term is more typically used to refer to a formerly living person or animal.

EVP, Electronic Voice Phenomena

EVPs are the unexplainable voices or sounds that are heard by investigators only when electronic recordings made during an investigation are played back. The entities that are responsible for these audible manifestations are typically nonthreatening and are usually not associated with any other physical manifestation that may be a cause for concern to occupants. Care must be taken by the audio specialist to ensure that these audio anomalies are not the noises or soft voices of other investigators or occupants farther away from the recorder.

GHOST

A ghost is the spirit of a dead person or animal believed to be associated with a specific location or object. Ghosts may present as physical apparitions, nonthreatening movement of objects or simply as audible effects such as taps, creaking noises, footsteps or as EVPs.

IMP

An imp is a malevolent entity that purposefully acts to harass occupants as well as investigators. Imps have a tendency to play tricks, pull pranks and repeatedly harass the occupants and paranormal investigators. They are able to cause a variety of minor damage to property, rearrange objects, move objects, create a variety of odors and occasionally start small fires. If an olfactory manifestation is present, the entity is probably an imp. While these entities are much less dangerous than demons, they still require the use of exorcists from a religious organization or a professional demonologist to exorcise them, and they should be avoided by occupants, researchers and investigators if at all possible.

MIST

Mist is an observable yet inexplicable phenomenon resembling a small cloud or haze that is believed to be made up of some sort of ectoplasm. When a mist is observed, it will quite often be accompanied by a localized cold spot. The mist is usually found to be several feet above the ground, and it may be found stationary or, less frequently, be moving around. As mist may perhaps be made up of ectoplasm, investigators will occasionally erroneously refer to mist as ectoplasm and tend to use the terms interchangeably.

ORB

An orb is a globe-shaped concentration of energy typically manifesting as white spots on photographs or in video taken of reportedly haunted locations. The filmmaker Fujifilm, on the company website, contradicted this definition by claiming that orbs that have been captured on the photographic images of paranormal researchers and others are not paranormal in nature—they probably are only particles of dust that are not in focus.[9]

The company went on to claim that these may also be reflections of the light flash of the camera when the photo was being taken. It is Fujifilm's contention that the close-up particles of dust are reflecting light better than particles that are farther away from the flash and would be seen as a circular blur on photographs.

The site also points out that raindrops are known to cause a similar effect, as does dust from construction.

In keeping with Fujifilm's opinion, small flying out-of-focus bugs could also appear as white spots on photographs and video recordings. Flying insects would also be able to change trajectory, as has been observed in many accounts of floating orbs. This rational and scientific explanation thoughtfully provided by Fujifilm does not, however, explain the higher EMF readings that are occasionally found with the appearance of orbs.

POLTERGEIST

The term *poltergeist* is a German expression that means "noisy ghost." This type of paranormal entity is typically identified as possessing only an audible presence or manifestation, and they have been found by researchers to be very nonthreatening, although the noises that are heard may be very disconcerting to those hearing them.

RESIDUAL HAUNTING

A residual haunting is a frequently recurring, nonthreatening, visible and/or audible manifestation that does not appear to have any purposeful action or thought. This is similar to watching or listening to a videotape or audiotape over and over. Residual haunting has also been known to be called after-echoes by some. Examples would be footsteps heard over and over on a stairway or in a hall, doorknobs that rattle periodically or apparitions seen performing the same actions again and again. An inanimate version of a residual haunting would be the ghostly appearance of the Flying Dutchman seen by sailors.

SHADOW PERSON

A shadow person is another term occasionally used to refer to a spirit.

SHADOWS

Shadows tend to present as dark apparitions that are usually very difficult to discern by eye. Typically, shadows are seen as translucent and are better observed on video or in photographs. Investigators may best be able to find shadows as motion seen out of the corners of their eyes. While shadows are not typically associated with other negative manifestations and tend to be able to utilize less ectoplasmic energy, they may be quite disconcerting to those observing them.

SPIRIT

A spirit is believed to be an entity that probably was not born an earthly creature such as a human or an animal. An example of an entity that may be considered to be a spirit would be an angel, a demon, a devil, a djinn and so on. These entities have also been referred to as shadow persons in a variety of literature. Spirits require the use of exorcists from a religious organization or a professional demonologist to exorcise them, and they should be avoided by occupants, researchers and investigators if at all possible

STREAK

A streak is an unexplained line of light that is captured on photographs and that is similar to an orb but is lengthened. A true streak would be made of ectoplasm and accompanied by high EMF readings. Investigators almost never report the presence of a streak during an investigation; they are found only during the review of the evidence collected during it. For this reason, they are typically explained away as camera movement during the taking of a photograph.

VORTEX

A vortex is defined as a small area of highly concentrated electromagnetic energy that may be captured in photographs taken during a paranormal investigation. A vortex has typically been found in the shape of a V or a rod and is normally associated with cold spots. Vortexes have been found in residences by investigators. There are theories that these may be the spirits of former residents or the physical manifestation of spirits traveling between dimensions.

20
Types of Manifestations

An Unexpected or Unidentifiable Noise Is Heard

If this kind of noise occurred in public and in the middle of the day, it is quite possible that it might easily go unnoticed or would cause little, if any, apprehension or alarm. At night, however, in a closed business, at a time when there are not supposed to be any other employees present, this identical noise could be very disconcerting to the individual hearing it.

Noises in buildings are to be expected in the normal course of events. Not everything that goes bump in the middle of the night is a ghost. It has been found that most creaks, groans, bumps, snaps and rattles have a perfectly reasonable and rational scientific explanation, and these noises can be indicative of a properly functioning building.

- One reasonable and rational scientific explanation for unusual noises would be the heating and cooling of materials, which cause expansion and contraction over time. The noises heard at night may just be the contraction of the building as it cools from the heat of the sun built up during the day.
- Another scientifically credible source for unusual noises is that buildings tend to settle over time, and the wind pushes on buildings and their various components, which can cause noise.

- Vibrations from passing vehicles, trucks and trains may cause vibration and stress inside buildings, which may result in the audible bumps, creaks or snaps that are heard.
- The activation of a piece of building equipment such as the air conditioner or heater turning on could be causing the unusual noise, especially if it is starting to deteriorate or malfunction. Even a fan becoming unbalanced could cause unusual noises that come and go.
- It is possible that the normal activities of neighbors or their possessions may be misinterpreted as the audible physical manifestations of entities if the buildings are located close together.

Audible noises without actual voices would be one of the lowest possible levels of paranormal activity, and as there are quite a few rational common explanations for them, they may well be disregarded by paranormal investigators if they are not found in the company of other, more physical manifestations.

An Apparent Motion Seen Only in the Corner of the Eye

C.A. Johnson, in a study published in the February 1986 *American Journal of Optometry and Physical Optics*, identified that motion detection in the peripheral vision of humans was superior to the ability to detect stationary objects even though it was inferior to the motion detection ability of the central vision. In other words, objects that are seen in the corner of the eye that have no relative motion are unlikely to be noticed by the observer, while objects that do display motion would be much more likely to be seen.[10]

Eyes are continuously scanning and forming a picture of what is perceived. Cones, primarily located in the center of eyes, provide for excellent detection of color and motion. Rods are the primary source of peripheral vision and tend to be more sensitive to light differences but are still able to detect relative motion.

Just because it is possible for motion to be detected out of the corner of the eye does not necessarily mean that there really is something moving. While this seems contradictory, there have been several scientific studies conducted to examine this phenomenon.

In 1999, Faubert and Herbert published a study in the journal *Perception* investigating how motion detected by the corner of the eye might be nothing more than an optical illusion. The phrase "peripheral drift illusion" was coined to refer to this type of motion illusion.[11]

Moving objects seen only in the corner of the eye of an investigator or building occupant are included on the lowest level of paranormal activity, as it may turn out to be nothing more than a peripheral drift illusion. This reported manifestation may well be disregarded by investigators if not found in the company of other physical manifestations.

FOOTSTEPS ARE HEARD WHEN NO ONE ELSE IS AROUND

The person hearing the footsteps should call the local police immediately. The odds are really good that the footsteps heard are not any form of a paranormal manifestation but that it is someone human like a burglar, vagrant or vandal who has entered the property and probably does not have good intentions toward either the occupants or their property.

There could be other natural or scientific explanations for the footsteps:

- Is there another residence or building close by that the footsteps that were heard could be coming from? A rational explanation for the footsteps heard could be that the buildings or residences were built too close together, or it could be they share a common wall; the footsteps could be just echoes coming from the other building or residence. The neighbors may also be found to have heavy feet. (Some people just can't be taught to walk softly.)
- Are the footsteps originating from an occupant or investigator in another room, hall or floor of the building? Acoustical properties of the building could possibly allow echoes of footsteps from elsewhere in a building to be heard.
- Is someone playing a prank, or is it a hoax? Pranks and hoaxes can happen. It is important for the investigator or occupant to check for speakers, sound tubes and so forth that would indicate how the hoax or prank was conducted.

Paranormal manifestations such as the minor movement or a stair stepping noise would require a small to medium expenditure of ectoplasmic energy to generate. These manifestations may be a one-time event or could be recurring. If they recur and sound the same each time, it is probably just a residual haunting that has no intelligent thought behind it. If the footsteps sound different each time they occur, there is a good chance the physical manifestation is being caused by an intelligent entity trying to communicate with the physical world. In either case, the manifestation would not usually pose a threat to the occupant or to an investigation team, though the footsteps may be disconcerting to the occupant hearing them.

A Door or Window that Opens or Closes Without Any Apparent Human Intervention

The first thing an occupant or investigator must do is to ensure there was no human intervention. A burglar, vagrant or vandal would need access to the building somehow, and a window or door is the most logical choice. If one of these has caused the occurrence, the investigator or occupant should call the police immediately.

If there was no apparent human intervention, other natural and scientific causes must be investigated prior to assigning it a paranormal cause. The following are examples of scientific and natural causes:

- Did the central air conditioner or heater fan just energize, causing air flow? The motion of the air caused by the fan could provide the required kinetic energy needed as an impetus to start the door or window into motion.
- Is it breezy outside? The air flow from the wind could provide the required kinetic energy that would be needed to start the door or window motion. Even if all other doors and windows are closed, buildings are not built to be impervious to air penetration. There has always been leakage into buildings of the exterior atmosphere, though the quantity permitted has been significantly reduced with modern construction's energy efficiency standards.
- Did another investigator or occupant open another door or window? The slight suction caused by the opening or

closing of another door or window in the building could potentially provide the required kinetic energy to cause the observed motion.

- Did someone energize an indoor fan? The suction caused by a bathroom fan or the air flow generated by a ceiling fan or a floor fan could potentially provide the required kinetic energy to cause the observed motion.
- Was something leaning against the window or door? An object leaning against the door or window may not generate sufficient kinetic energy to start the motion immediately. Energy is cumulative. An imperceptible earth movement, the settling of the building or even the vibrations caused by the occupants' or researchers' footsteps could add sufficient additional energy to start the motion of the door or window. Once motion has been started, less energy (such as that provided by the original object leaning against the door or window) is required to maintain or to accelerate the motion.
- Is the door level? A door that is not hung level will have a propensity to swing. It may not have sufficient kinetic energy to start on its own, but as before, an almost imperceptible earth movement, the settling of the building or even the vibrations caused by the occupants' or researchers' footsteps could add sufficient additional energy to start the motion of the door.
- Is the house level? As before, a residence that is not level may give doors the tendency to swing on their own when just a little more impetus is given by an almost imperceptible earth movement, the settling of the building or even the vibrations caused by the occupants' or researchers' footsteps.
- Is someone playing a prank or is it a hoax? Pranks and hoaxes can happen. It is important for the investigator or occupant to check for hooks, weights, thin wire and such that would indicate how the hoax or prank was conducted.

If no natural or scientific explanation is apparent, EMF readings in the vicinity would tend to confirm the presence of a paranormal entity. The kinetic energy required of a paranormal entity to begin to move a door or window is not an excessive amount, but the EMF signature would be detectable by investigators' instruments. A temperature variation may also occur (cold spot) in the vicinity of the moving door or window as the entity may be converting thermal energy into kinetic energy. If no EMF signature is present and no cold spot is apparent, it is recommended the investigator reexamine all possible natural and scientific causes.

A Shadow Seen Where None Should Be

If it is seen only out of the corner of the eye, vanishes when looked at directly and is not accompanied by an increased level of EMF readings or a temperature variation (hot or cold spot), this manifestation should be disregarded by investigators and may be labeled peripheral drift illusion.

If there is a stationary or moving shadow observed, natural and scientific explanations should be examined before claiming it was generated by a paranormal presence:

- Are the shadows coming from outside a window? It is possible the moon has come out from behind a cloud and the shadows are from the trees or bushes outside the building.
- Was a vehicle passing by outside? Even through closed blinds, the light cast from the headlights of a passing vehicle could possibly cast shadows into a room
- Is there an investigator or occupant outside with a light? Like a vehicle's headlights, a flashlight beam cast on the side of a building under investigation may cause shadows to be seen in a room.
- Are the shadows from an investigator's or occupant's light source inside the residence? Light sources in other rooms should be checked to see if they may be causing the shadow. Even the LED lights of an EMF detector can cast shadow
- Is someone playing a prank or is it a hoax? Pranks and hoaxes can happen. It is important for the investigator or occupant to check for any possible hidden light sources that would indicate how the hoax or prank was pulled off.

If no rational or scientific explanation is found, investigators should check for temperature variations and EMF readings. Shadows tend to expend less ectoplasmic energy to manifest than would a full apparition, but the signature higher EMF levels associated with paranormal activity should be present. As these beings are less able to utilize energy to manifest and may be translucent to the point of almost invisibility, it may be easier to observe them on video or in still photographs.

As these entities seem able to handle only limited amounts of ectoplasmic energy to provide physical manifestations, they would seem to not pose much of a threat to the investigator or the occupant but may be discomforting to have around.

A LIGHT OR GLOWING OBJECT SEEN WHERE NONE SHOULD BE

The majority of reports of lights, orbs and glowing objects floating in the air have the objects in question located away from a building or structure. If the glowing light or orb is in the sky, it may be only a firefly, a plane, a helicopter, a military flare, swamp gas or a UFO. It may also be some sort of a paranormal ectoplasmic entity, but it may be a little difficult for investigators to gather much evidence on unless it comes down to earth.

Paranormal investigators are much more likely to encounter orbs or other glowing objects indoors. As previously presented, Fujifilm has determined that orbs that are observed on photographs or video recordings are merely light reflection on out-of-focus particles of dust. This may well be, since paranormal investigators rarely observe the orbs personally, and EMF readings remain stable while the orbs are present. Alternately, that some of the orbs that are recorded on photographs and video are nothing more than out-of-focus flying insects also is a plausible explanation.

A visible light, orb or glowing object that is observed by an investigator and confirmed on film might make it a little more difficult to identify a natural or scientific cause.

If there is a glowing object observed, there are some natural and scientific explanations that should be examined before claiming it was generated by a paranormal presence:

- The observed light phenomena could be just a reflection of another illumination source being refracted off of a mirror or another shiny surface.
- The glowing balls could be some form of ball lightning. Ball lightning is a type of atmospheric electrical phenomena not

usually associated with thunderstorms. Reports have them being anywhere from marble sized to the size of armchairs and are quite often reported to have been sighted inside a building. These glowing balls have been reported to move up and down, side to side, stay stationary or any combination. The balls could slowly dissipate, vanish suddenly or even explode loudly. The only things all ball lightning has in common is that it appears to be bright orbs, electrical in nature, and generates an extremely large EMF reading.

- The glowing balls could be some form of ignited swamp gas. Outdoors, near a swamp and with a highly charged atmosphere, this may be a possible explanation. If it is found indoors with no smell of gas (the artificial smell added to natural gas), this explanation would be extremely unlikely.

The scientific descriptions and explanations given of ball lightning seem to closely fit those of a paranormal entity's manifestations, a floating ball of energy that is visible, glows and gives off a lot of EMF. It usually appears without warning and can go away quietly or with a big bang. By the scientific descriptions, scientists could well be trying to explain away the various appearances of paranormal entities.

Items Found in Different Locations than Where They Were Left

Many reports have been made of objects being repositioned within a building without human intervention. These reports rarely include any additional physical manifestations that would typically accompany any activity of this sort by an actual paranormal entity.

- The most probable scientific and rational explanation for the object not being found in the location they were reportedly left is the memory of the person reporting the occurrence. They may have thought they put something where they had claimed but had actually placed it somewhere else (probably where they found it).
- Another scientific and rational explanation would be that someone else in the residence or business picked the object

up, used it and then set it down somewhere other than where they originally got it from without telling the first person.
- It is possible that it could be a house pet that moved the object. Dogs and especially cats have the tendency to pick up objects that attract their attention, play with them for a little while and then leave them elsewhere when they get tired of playing. Despite years of research and experiments, scientists have yet to find an effective method of getting dogs and cats to clean up after themselves and put their toys back where they found them.
- A fairly simple means of determining if Fluffy or Fido was the culprit and moved the item in question would be to check the object that was moved for the residual presence of saliva. Saliva is characteristically different from an ectoplasmic residue, as the ectoplasm will rapidly dissipate into the air or into the object, whereas saliva will leave an obvious slimy residue.
- If the object is round and appears to roll by itself, the explanation could be as simple as an uneven or unlevel floor or table surface. This is easily confirmed by placing a ball bearing or marble on the same surface. If the ball bearing or marble rolls in the same direction as the object rolled, the surface is probably not level.
- The final reasonable and rational explanations are that either a co-worker or another occupant is playing a prank or hoax on the person reporting the activity, or the person reporting the paranormal relocation of the object is fabricating the entire story.

If the object was repositioned by a paranormal entity, it would have required an extraordinarily high expenditure of ectoplasmic energy on the part of the paranormal entity. This large energy expenditure may have caused a cold spot in the room or could have caused the building's lights to flicker or dim. It would also result in extremely high and fluctuating EMF readings on a detector. These secondary physical manifestations would tend to provide the investigator with supporting evidence to the assertion that the reported activity was paranormal in nature.

Unusual Unexplainable Odors, Such as Perfume, Smoke, Sulfur

Reports have been made of a variety of inexplicable olfactory manifestations that reportedly are not of human origin. If these reports are not accompanied by any secondary or supporting paranormal activity, which most are not, they would not usually be given a high priority for commencing a complete paranormal investigation.

- The scientific and rational explanations to explain odors are abundant. They can come from someone right outside of a window or a door; they could have been retained in walls, ceilings, floors, insulation, furniture, clothing and so forth and just be a residual smell from the current or previous occupants. Pet odors such as urine smell have been found to be extremely difficult to eradicate after someone moves out. Likewise, the odor of smoke from a fire has been found to permeate substances and to be released over time.
- Noticeable odors are able to be spread by circulating fans, air conditioning, even by a breeze that is blowing outside. Exterior surfaces are required to have a specified maximum permeability to the passage of air, which means the scent may be coming through a wall without windows or doors.
- The odor that is detected by the investigator could even have been brought to the investigation site on the equipment or clothing of the investigators themselves. Most people are able to identify the odor of smoke emanating from the clothing of a smoker.
- It is possible the occupant is deliberately attempting to perpetrate a hoax on the investigators and has deliberately placed material in the building that has a residual odor or smell.
- It is possible that the odor being smelled is just a physical manifestation of withdrawal from alcohol or some pharmaceuticals. If the report is coming from an occupant, this must be seriously considered. If it is an investigator reporting it, it may be more credible, especially if accompanied by high EMF readings.

The paranormal manifestation of an observed noticeable odor is usually just a byproduct of some other physical manifestation, such as the appearance of an apparition. The energy required for the odor would be a small portion of the ectoplasmic energy required to be expended to generate the appearance of the apparition. This type of manifestation by itself is one of the least likely to be hoaxed.

Of all of the human senses, smell is one of the least effective pieces of evidence that can be observed. There is no method available to retain the odors reported by the occupants or the investigators. While smell may be useful as a potential form of supporting evidence to back up another form of a paranormal physical manifestation, it is useless as the primary.

Lights Turning Off and On Without Human Intervention

There have been very few reported paranormal occurrences of lights turning on and off without someone operating the switch. Although it may be rare, it is possible for these manifestations to occur.

- The most common rational and scientific explanation for the lights that operate without someone touching the switch is the lights are activated by a motion or pressure sensor. The motion sensor may be incorporated into the body of the light (such as an exterior motion sensing light fixture) or may be embedded into the switch itself. If it is operated by a motion sensor, it may be obvious or well concealed. Pressure sensors have been used in expensive intrusion detection systems but are able to be adapted to activate lights, recording devices, even sound generators.
- If there is no motion or pressure sensor found, another reasonable and rational explanation would be an electrical fault in the wiring, in the breaker, in the switch or in the light fixture itself. An electrician should immediately be consulted, as this may be caused by a high-resistance connection that is overheating. A high-resistance condition may eventually result in either a failure of the circuit or in a fire in the building. Electrical causes have been found to be the leading cause of fires in buildings.

- It is always a really good idea for the investigator to check to see if the operation of the light is being caused by surreptitious human intervention. A three-way switch could have been installed elsewhere in the building, or there could even be a remote control device that is being operated by a co-conspirator to provide the impression to the investigator that the light was being operated by a paranormal entity.

While there are quite a few scientific explanations for lights turning on and off, it may well be a paranormal entity restricting or allowing the flow of electricity either manually (operating a switch) or by diverting the energy for its own use in another type of physical manifestation. Typically, the ectoplasmic energy use required for an entity to create a physical manifestation should only cause the lights to flicker or perhaps dim, but complete diversion of the electrical energy is possible. The amount of ectoplasmic energy conversion required to completely and totally extinguish a light should be able to light up investigators' EMF meters at quite a distance. It might be better to leave the entity alone or turn it over to a professional exorcist.

Areas that Seem Abnormally Hot or Cold Without the Heat or Air Being On

The temperature of the air is a detectable and recordable indication of the kinetic energy of the particles that make up the air. Temperature is the detectable property of the speed of motion (kinetic energy) of the particles that make up an object (such as air). The use or conversion of ectoplasmic energy can be drawn from the thermodynamic properties of the air in a room. The conversion of this thermal or kinetic energy to ectoplasmic energy would remove a portion of the kinetic energy from the air, causing the particles to slow down and make it feel colder. This thermal property of the air can be detected by a non-contact thermometer. Entities may also convert the thermal or kinetic energy of material objects (such as walls) into ectoplasmic energy to manifest. This change in temperature of a material object can be detected by non-contact thermometers.

A temperature reading that is higher or rises might be caused by the presence of an entity that is converting other energies into thermal or kinetic energy. This can result in unexplained fires or hot surfaces that can discomfort or burn an occupant or researcher.

- The most probable reasonable and rational scientific explanation for the detection of a colder or warmer temperature or a temperature reading that is changing perceptibly would be the activation of the building's heating or air conditioning equipment. The starting of a ceiling fan or an oscillating fan could also easily prove to be the cause of the observed phenomena.
- Another reasonable explanation for a change in temperature could be air from another part of the building flowing into the room being monitored. This airflow would result in thermal cross contamination of the area being observed. For example, an investigator opening or closing a window or door in the room in question or even in another room could result in an air exchange with an adjacent room or the outside atmosphere. The air that was injected into the room could be at a different temperature than the temperature of the air that preexisted in the room, and this would show up as an increasing or decreasing thermal reading.
- A change in the detected temperature of a wall or other surface could be caused by the temperature of the space beyond it changing over time. An exterior wall can be affected by both the ambient temperature of the outside air and by the radiant energy of the sun (or lack thereof if the sun just went down or is covered by a cloud). This temperature gradient within the wall is affected by the insulation resistance of the material composition of the wall. This means that the less insulated the wall is, the more that the changes in the exterior wall temperature will affect the interior surface.
- The change in instrument-indicated thermal conditions could be just an equipment malfunction or a sign the batteries are going dead. The readings can be confirmed by the investigator holding the detector sensing the temperature change as well as observing the change in readings on the instrument.

If the change in thermal conditions is caused by a paranormal manifestation converting thermal energy to ectoplasmic energy, it should also be accompanied by higher than normal EMF readings in the area in which the temperature changed. This is a type of manifestation that is one of the least likely to be hoaxed.

The Hairs on the Back of the Neck Rising for No Apparent Reason

The hairs on the surface of the human body are able to react to the surrounding environment by rising under several different circumstances without the need for paranormal intervention.

- One reasonable and rational scientific explanation would be a change in temperature. An investigator or occupant entering an air-conditioned space from a warmer environment has a chance of developing goose bumps. These are a normal physical reaction of the human body's skin to increase the thermal shielding of the body in an attempt to retain body heat. This is a primitive holdover from long ago when humans' bodies were covered by a much thicker fur.
- Another reasonable explanation is another primitive holdover reaction of the skin to perceived danger. If a human body (even unconsciously) believes it may be in danger, the skin reacts similarly to if it feels cold. The hair rises in a similar manner to the hackles on Fido or the fur on Fluffy puffing out when facing a dangerous situation. The increased depth of hair makes the frightened creature seem larger than they really are, which might cause an attacker to think twice about attacking. This unconscious reaction does not have any practical purpose with humans other than giving the individual an awareness of the subconscious concern for the existing conditions.
- An unlikely but possible rational cause could be the presence of a high electromagnetic field such as that found directly under high power lines. Most buildings are not built under high power lines, but if they were, the entire residence would

display similar if not the same characteristic high EMF readings. This cause can be eliminated if there are no high power lines near the residence.

Another cause could be paranormal activity. Paranormal manifestations that generate EMF may be felt by rising hair on the skin if the generated electromagnetic field is strong enough. The hair rising would be good for a secondary indication to confirm other more obvious physical manifestations caused by an entity. This is one type of manifestation that is almost impossible to hoax.

PETS START ACTING DIFFERENTLY THAN NORMAL

Fluffy and Fido have been found by researchers to be able to detect many things that normal human beings are typically insensitive to. Just because the pets in the house are acting stranger than normal does not provide absolute proof that an entity has taken up residence and is manifesting.

- One reasonable and rational scientific explanation is that the pets could be sensing low amplitude vibrations that most human beings are not able to sense. These low amplitude vibrations have been found by scientists to be precursors to detectable tectonic activity (earthquakes).
- Another possible explanation is that indoor pets can get a form of cabin fever the same as humans do. This can generate feelings of uneasiness and anxiety. The resultant increase in adrenalin can result in excess activity and abnormal activity.
- This activity on the part of Fido or Fluffy could be just part of an elaborate hoax perpetrated by the owner, tenant or co-conspirator. Having another person stationed in another room or outside with an ultrasonic whistle that produces a sound above the investigators' threshold of hearing could get the animal(s) aggravated and active without the investigator suspecting anything.

Pets acting strangely cannot be accurately quantified or measured. It is possible that the actions of the pets are due to a paranormal manifestation that only the animals can sense. Researchers have determined that dogs and cats are able to hear ultrasonic and subsonic sounds and see in a wider spectrum of light than human beings. While dogs are sensitive to entities and will bark, growl or whine with their tails between their legs in the presence of an entity, cats seem to be fearless. Fluffy will attempt to actively play with, pursue and chase the entity around and away from the residence. It almost seems like some manifested entities are afraid of cats.

A FEELING OF DREAD COMING OVER SOMEONE WITH NO APPARENT CAUSE

Feelings of dread are a normal body's reaction to a subconscious awareness of danger, similar to the hair raising on the back of the neck.

- One reasonable and scientific explanation would be that something in the surrounding environment that may be below the threshold of the normal human senses has caused the body of the occupant or investigator to become apprehensive.
- Another reasonable explanation is that the occupant or investigator has somehow mentally caused their own apprehension, and the feeling of dread has nothing to do with a paranormal manifestation.
- It is also possible that the feeling of dread is just a physical manifestation of withdrawal from alcohol or some pharmaceuticals. If the report of the feeling is coming from an occupant, this must be seriously considered. If it is an investigator reporting it, it may be more credible, especially if accompanied by higher EMF readings.

While a feeling of dread might be a good secondary piece of evidence for the presence of a paranormal entity, it would be insufficient as a primary source. If the feeling was accompanied by higher EMF readings, the EMF readings would be the primary evidence, with the feelings of dread backing it up as secondary evidence.

A feeling of dread would not require a significant amount of ectoplasmic energy use and may not require continuous use, but the energy in the form of EMF could be found in detectable quantities.

Electronic Voice Phenomena (EVP)

Audio recordings and sometimes video recordings with audio are quite often recorded by occupants and investigators. When these recordings are played back, there are sometimes additional voices that were not audible to people present when the recording was made. These low-level sounds could be a paranormal manifestation, or there could be a more mundane explanation.

- The most probable reasonable and rational scientific explanation would be the voices that are heard on the recording are other occupants or other investigators who are in an adjacent room or hall or just outside the building. The voices detected are usually softer than the other voices, and this would be consistent with it being generated by individuals who are farther away from the recording device.
- The voices that are recorded could possibly be a manifestation caused deliberately by the owner, occupant or some other co-conspirator attempting to perpetrate a hoax. There could be a secreted speaker and microphone linking the room to an individual who could be miles away. The remote individual could provide soft responses the investigator might not be able to hear but would be picked up and discovered later on an audio recorder. A radio frequency (RF) detector will typically be able to detect and indicate the broadcast and return transmission for the hidden microphone and speaker.

Barring any reasonable explanation. it could be a paranormal entity attempting to communicate with the investigator. The quantity of ectoplasmic energy that would need to be expended by a paranormal entity to receive, understand and respond to voices would be slightly less than the amount required to form an apparition.

Disembodied Voices

The person hearing the voices should call the local police immediately, as they should do when they hear footsteps when no one is supposed to be around. It is much more likely that the voices and/or footsteps are not being caused by a paranormal entity but are being generated by burglars, vagrants or vandals.

- Assuming the investigator has determined the voices are not caused by humans in the building without permission, the voices that are being heard may be originating from just outside the building or from a nearby residence or building, especially if the buildings were built close together or the neighbors have loud voices or their television volume is set on high.
- The voices that are heard could possibly be a manifestation caused deliberately by the owner, occupant or some other co-conspirator attempting to perpetrate a hoax. There could be a secreted speaker and microphone linking the room to an individual who could be miles away. The remote individual could provide an interactive conversation with the investigator. An RF detector will typically be able to detect and indicate the broadcast and return transmission for the hidden microphone and speaker.

Interactive paranormal manifestations that are audible to the human ear are nowhere near as common as are visual manifestations or EVPs, as louder sounds would require the expenditure of much more ectoplasmic energy to generate. An entity that is able to directly communicate verbally and interact with an investigator without the need for the investigator to use EVP or EMF detectors would need to be a fairly powerful phantasm expending a reasonably large amount of energy.

If the words that are heard by the investigator or occupant are something like "Leave," "Get out!" or "Go away!," the individual hearing the words should not stick around and argue with the entity. Anything with that much energy, that has clearly demonstrated a negative opinion to a human presence, may decide to encourage the individuals' speedy departure if the individuals hesitate. With the ability to convert that much energy, the entity could probably cause material objects to accelerate rapidly toward the occupants or investigator or perhaps even physically accelerate the investigator or occupants through a window, a wall or even through a closed door, much to the detriment of the individuals affected.

Physical Contact When No One Else Is Around

The sense of being touched by something is not an unusual occurrence. People are touched by things every day of their lives. The skin is very sensitive to pressure and is capable of detecting some sound waves, heat, cold and other forms of energy.

- A simple scientific and rational explanation would be that the individual reporting being touched had merely brushed up against a material object and did not believe they were as close to it as they really were.
- Another possible scientific explanation for the feeling of being touched or brushed up against is that it actually occurred. Fluffy's tail brushing up against an investigator's arm or leg can be very disconcerting if the investigator doesn't know the pet is there and is not expecting it. An investigator's frightened reaction could also cause Fluffy to rapidly depart the scene, leaving only a paranormal explanation for the investigator. The rapid departure of Fluffy could also cause unexpected and unexplained noise that might be attributed erroneously by the investigator as the manifestation of an entity. It would be important for the investigator to ensure no pets are present, especially for a lights-out investigation.
- Another physical cause of an investigator feeling touched would be the presence of flying insects. It would behoove the investigator to look around and try to see if there are any flying insects, moths and so forth inside the building with them.
- The scientific culprit behind the investigator feeling touched could just be cobwebs. When an investigator moves around in a spooky old building, they may forget about the possibility that spiders have been there for a long time before them. It would be important for investigators to note the presence and location of all cobwebs prior to beginning a lights-out investigation.
- Some investigations are performed in places that may not be as clean as investigators would like. It is possible the touch sensation is only the feet of spiders, ants, caterpillars, centipedes, bedbugs and even fleas if Fido or Fluffy live in the building. It is important for an investigator who feels

touched to have another investigator look at the area before the investigator brushes at it. Unfortunately, it is only human instinct to brush at a location on the body that seems to sense something unusual present.

- The feeling of being touched or having something crawl on an individual is also a physical manifestation of withdrawal from alcohol or some pharmaceuticals. If the report is coming from an occupant, this must be seriously considered. If it is an investigator reporting it, it may be more credible, especially if marks are left by the entity.

While there are quite a few reasonable and rational scientific explanations for an occupant or investigator reporting having been touched, standing alone, this manifestation would not be scientifically credible to determining the presence of a paranormal entity, due to the inability of instruments to detect the touch on the human skin.

If an entity were manifesting at a sufficient level to actually be able to touch someone, it would have to be using a reasonably large amount of detectable ectoplasmic energy. This use of ectoplasmic energy would be detectable on EMF meters by the investigators. This detectable level of EMF readings would tend to support the report of the investigator of having been touched. In this case the detected EMF readings would be the primary indicator and evidence of the presence of a paranormal entity and the touch would be used as supporting evidence.

The Sudden Appearance of an Apparition

The sudden appearance of an apparition can be extremely disconcerting to an occupant or investigator. While these have been reported, they are rarely caught on camera or video. The reasons given for the apparition not being photographed are varied. The reasons given include those such as the camera was pointed in the wrong direction, the paranormal apparition disappeared before a camera could be brought around to photograph it and the batteries in the camera went dead.

- One reasonable and scientific explanation for the appearance and disappearance of an apparition would be that it was merely the reflection in a mirror or glass of someone or something else in the room. If the mirror or glass moved or if the object moved, it could be reported as an apparition.

- The apparition could be a hoax perpetrated by the owner or occupant seeking attention. The apparition could have been projected onto a wall, mirror or glass by a secreted projector operated by the occupant or a co-conspirator.

An actual apparition caught on video or photograph would be ideal as primary evidence of the presence of a paranormal entity and a haunting. This will normally be accompanied by a high EMF reading on the investigators' detector, as the amount of ectoplasmic energy required for an entity to materialize is significant.

This type of scientific evidence is part of the ultimate goal of paranormal investigators, multiple forms of irrefutable proof pointing toward the actual presence of a paranormal entity. The only thing that would make this better would be capturing the audible interactions of the investigator with the paranormal entity.

A Physical Attack on an Occupant or Investigator

A physical attack on an investigator or occupant is an extremely dangerous occurrence. A simple physical manifestation would require a large amount of ectoplasmic energy to be expended by an entity, but that amount would be nothing compared to the amount required to be expended for an actual physical attack on a human.

Anything that has demonstrated the ability to use that much energy and that has clearly demonstrated a negative opinion to the presence of an investigator or occupant is nothing to be trifled with casually. The entity may decide to encourage the individuals' rapid departure if the individual appears to hesitate or not demonstrate an expeditious withdrawal. With the ability to convert that much ectoplasmic energy, the paranormal entity could possibly cause material objects to accelerate rapidly toward the occupants or investigator or could perhaps even physically accelerate the investigator or occupant through a window, a wall or through a closed door, which would be very detrimental to the future well-being of the individual affected.

In the event there is an actual attack on an investigator or an occupant, it would be best to turn over such entities to the careful ministrations of exorcists representing a religious organization or to a professional demonologist, and the paranormal entity should be avoided by occupants, researchers and investigators if at all possible.

21
Makeup of a Paranormal Research Group

Paranormal research groups are many and varied. Some are simply a couple of individuals with an EMF detector and too much spare time. At the other end of the spectrum are professionally organized groups made up of dozens of people utilizing commonly accepted scientific methods, top-of-the-line equipment and a fairly large amount of financial resources.

There are big differences between a paranormal research group and a ghost hunting group. Ghost hunters go to places that are likely to be haunted and look for evidence supporting the manifestations that may or may not be there. Paranormal research groups go to specific locations that have reported paranormal manifestations and attempt to identify and make contact with the entities that are producing the physically observed phenomena. Ghost hunters are typically found to be disorganized and poorly financed with only basic detection devices and have individuals with little experience dealing with the paranormal. Paranormal research groups tend to be better organized, have better financial resources, have a wider variety of paranormal detection and recording devices and have a combination of experienced and relatively inexperienced team members. Ghost hunters do it more for the fun of it, while paranormal researchers attempt to provide irrefutable scientific evidence to support their findings.

The key ingredient to a successful and productive paranormal investigation team is good, solid investigative techniques. Only by using proper and organized scientific processes to discretely document paranormal manifestations would it be possible to identify possible explanations for the observed activity or to document the reality of the paranormal activity.

Science is the systematic, repeatable observation of a variety of physical manifestations and the attempt to theorize explanations and predictions that would account for all of the observable phenomena regarding a specific event, occurrence or activity. Since the word *paranormal* means "beyond the normal," the systematic and scientific research conducted by paranormal researchers using standardized processes assist in determining both the existence and the parameters of the disembodied spirits being studied. This research may eventually result in the paranormal activity becoming the norm.

TEAM LEADER

The team leader acts as a supervisor to ensure all tasks are assigned to the appropriate individuals and all of the tasks that are assigned are satisfactorily performed. He or she keeps the process moving smoothly from the initial contact with the client by the contact manager to the completion of the investigation and examination of evidence collected during the investigation. The team leader's role is similar to the conductor of an orchestra. A conductor must orchestrate a multitude of different individuals playing a variety of different instruments into one harmonious and pleasant melody. Just like the conductor, the team's supervisor must orchestrate a variety of different people who utilize a multitude of different talents, sensors and recording devices to produce a final result of a reasonable and acceptable level of scientific investigation.

INVESTIGATOR

The investigators are the brave individuals involved in the actual attempt to detect and/or record the physical manifestations associated with the reported paranormal activity. These individuals are the backbone of the team, the people tasked with detecting and identifying the physical manifestations that may indicate the presence of a paranormal entity and to hopefully make contact and have some type of interaction with it. They are also responsible for recording all of their actions, equipment readings and personal observations on an investigation.

Debunker

Debunkers are the individual or individuals responsible for finding reasonable and rational scientific explanations for the observed or recorded abnormal phenomena and manifestations. They are responsible for weeding out the non-paranormal phenomena from the actual inexplicable paranormal entities' activities. Typically, debunkers come from scientific backgrounds, but the biggest requirement is that they have an unusually large amount of common sense and the firm belief that everything that is observable must have a rational and scientific explanation. An individual who professes not to believe in the supernatural would probably make the best debunker, but it is difficult to get someone who is not a true believer to join a paranormal investigation group or to become a part of one without an excessive amount of ridicule.

Client

The client is the person or persons reporting paranormal activity. While not technically a member of the paranormal research team, they are the stakeholder who is most affected by the outcome. They primarily interact with the contact manager and provide information on the physical manifestations observed as well as any history of the property that may be relevant. Relevant information includes any information concerning alcohol and/or drug use when the phenomena were observed.

Case/Contact Manager

The case, or contact, manager is the person who is the primary point of contact for the client. The case manager is responsible for interviewing the client and identifying any relevant information on the physical manifestations observed by the client and the history of the property. It will usually be necessary for the contact manager to interview all of the members of the family (if a residence) or employees (if a business). The contact manager assists the team leader in determining the resources required to adequately investigate the reported phenomena.

RESEARCHER/HISTORIAN

While the contact manager would be the one who interacts with the client(s), the researcher or historian (the terms are interchangeable) will look for records dealing with the property or the individuals involved. Public records will provide former owner information and any reported unusual events that may have occurred at the property. Years ago, this background investigation entailed weeks of searching old newspaper archives or research at a county clerks' office and pouring over old recorded land records. Modern methods such as internet searches typically make this much less time consuming but may still require visits to record offices. It has been found that a structure or facility that was built on top of an old Native American burial ground or on the site of a large bloody battle would be much more likely to have true paranormal activity. Family and personal information can also be important information vital to a successful investigation. When a diagnosed paranoid schizophrenic reports seeing abnormal things and/or hearing voices, it cannot immediately be assumed that it is due to the presence or physical manifestation of paranormal entities.

EQUIPMENT TECHNICIAN

The equipment technician(s) are responsible for the maintenance, operation and repair of all of the team's communally owned paranormal investigation equipment. This responsibility could include the handling of everything from the surveillance equipment, the equipment trailer and the electrical generator, even up to the wiring and positioning of the video recording surveillance equipment.

Audio Specialist

The audio specialist(s) are typically the investigators best trained in isolating and identifying audible paranormal phenomena. This role may also include analyzing EVP phenomena but usually entails working strictly with the noises that are within the audible range of the investigators' normal hearing. The audio specialist(s) are also tasked with ensuring the detected anomalies are not self-generated (generated by the equipment being used to record the audio or made by other investigators talking on scene) or were fabricated by either an investigator or the client. The audio specialist may double as the EVP specialist in smaller groups.

Video Specialist

The video specialist(s) are the individual(s) tasked with reviewing client-provided or investigator-gathered video evidence. They are responsible for analyzing the data provided looking for apparent anomalies. They are then required to determine if there may be a natural cause for the anomaly or if it could be a fabrication. The video specialist may double as the photographic specialist in smaller groups.

Photographic Specialist

The photographic specialist(s) are the individual(s) responsible for reviewing all of the photographic evidence that is provided by the client or that is collected by the investigators during an investigation. The photographic specialist may double as the video specialist and even the tech specialist in smaller groups.

EVP Specialist

The EVP specialist(s) are typically the investigators best trained in EVP phenomena. They are the ones who are trained on the use of the specialized audio software that is used to isolate extremely low abnormal electronic readings. They are also the ones who have the ability to discern soft entity-generated voices from the white noise background. They (as well as the audio specialist) are also tasked with ensuring detected anomalies are not self-generated (generated by the equipment being used to record audio or made by other investigators talking on scene) or were fabricated by either an investigator or the client.

22
Paranormal Investigation Tools

There is no comprehensive list of materials that will guarantee an investigation will result in positive results. There are, however, some basic materials that are readily available that will enable even the most economically distressed investigation team to get into ghost hunting adventures. To conserve and stretch funds as much as possible, pawnshops have been found to provide much needed financial relief. Digital cameras and video cameras (including ones with infrared lights), thermometers, walkie-talkies, compasses, audio recorders, tripods and even motion-activated infrared game cameras can be found at a significant discount off of retail price (up to 90 percent off retail has been found).

Investigation tools will be listed in order of the approximate or estimated retail price, with the least expensive items being listed first.

Ball Bearing

A ball bearing is useful to the investigator to determine if a floor or surface is level. A building that settles may end up with surfaces that are not level and may be one of the causes for doors or windows that swing open or closed as well as balls and other objects that are found to move across a floor without human intervention. Placing a ball bearing on the floor and allowing it to roll would give an indication of whether or not the floor is level. If the floor is level, that is one less rational and scientific explanation for the paranormal activity observed. Estimated cost is under $1.

Pencils/Pens and Notebooks

Pens and/or pencils are needed to record contact information, permission slips (the occupant or owner's authorization required to permit an investigation to be conducted), research efforts, questions or comments that may crop up during an investigation and investigation results. Finding a fluctuation in temperature or EMF readings is important but meaningless unless the values are accurately recorded. Estimated cost is between $5 and $20.

Flashlight

Flashlights are important to prevent accidents. It is preferable to have red lens installed on the flashlights to allow the investigators to retain their night vision. Estimated cost is $5 to $20.

Spare Batteries

Entities typically use some form of external energy for their manifestations. Sometimes they can use thermal energy, and sometimes they will use the chemical energy that is generated by batteries. The depletion of energy in batteries is one of the less obvious physical manifestations indicative of the presence of entities, but it can be extremely irritating to the investigator who fails to bring along spare batteries. Estimated cost is $10 to $30.

Cellphone

Cellphones are only needed prior to the start of an investigation and on-site only in case an emergency arises. Cellphones should not be allowed to be brought into the building being investigated due to the possibility the transmissions may be misidentified as an entity's manifestations of an electromagnetic energy field on a detector. As most individual investigators should already have personal cellphones, no expense should be incurred.

First Aid Kit

Unbelievable as it may seem, everyone is human, and everyone, at one time or another, had an accident. While most accidents that occur tend to be minor, it is important to keep a basic first aid kit with the investigation team or in one of the vehicles outside to tend to those minor injuries that may crop up. Estimated cost is $10 to $40.

Compass

A simple magnetic compass may give a physical indication of potential paranormal manifestations. Some types of entities have been reported to have a magnetic component that would cause the needle of the magnetic compass to swing off of true north. The compass's needle may point to the wrong location of north, or it may swing back and forth as if uncertain as to which magnetic source to point at. This abnormal shifting and movement of the needle may provide corroborating evidence for any other observed or recorded physical phenomena to suggest the presence of a paranormal entity. Estimated cost is $10 to $70.

Watch

Watches are important to the investigation so the time of occurrences can be accurately annotated. Watches and the correct time would be important to provide evidence of a commonality of occurrence. For example, EMF fluctuations are noted by an investigator with no other visual evidence observed. In the later evidence review, floating orbs are discovered on the digital photographs taken at the same time and at the same location. The

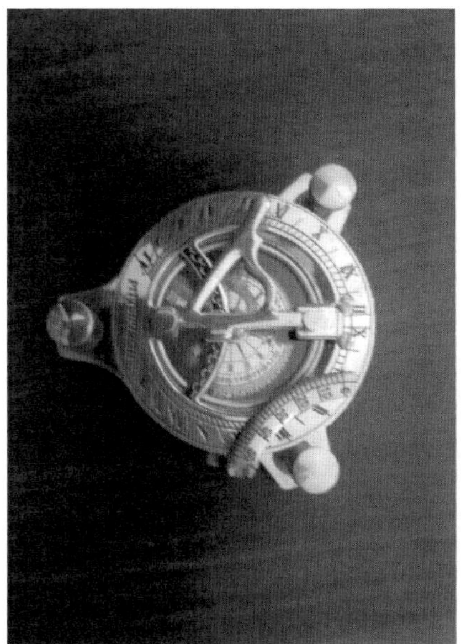

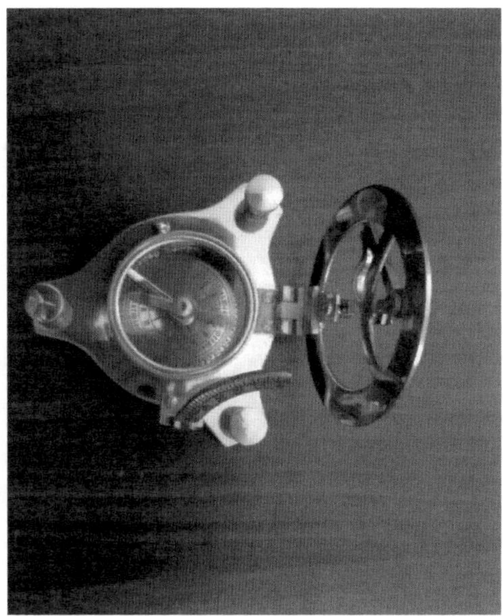

Left: Unusual-looking compass. *Right*: Open compass.

recording of the EMF fluctuations at the same time as the orbs would be corroborating evidence to suggest an entity was manifesting. Estimated cost is $10 to $100.

CAMERA TRIPODS

Small tripods are used to set up small video (infrared or regular) or audio recorders on tables or countertops. Estimated cost is $15 to $30.

Large tripods are useful for setting up and holding the infrared video cameras that would be required in a comprehensive investigation video monitoring system. The monitoring system would typically be set up by the video and technical specialist inside the building to give an overall view of anything that may occur. The video system would then be monitored by the video specialist who would be stationed in a trailer or vehicle located just outside the area under investigation. Large camera tripods are estimated to cost $15 to $35.

RF Detectors

Radio frequency signal detectors can be a vital asset to ensure the conducting of a more scientifically accurate paranormal investigation. These RF detectors are not primarily used to detect paranormal entities but instead are used to weed out potential hoaxes. When a radio frequency signal is detected, it means someone is broadcasting something.

The detected signal could have a reasonable and rational explanation. It could be an occupant's or investigator's cellphone or walkie-talkie transmitting. It could also be a wireless alarm or video surveillance system transmission. It may turn out that a disembodied voice that is being heard by investigators may be just someone using a hidden wireless speaker to fake the manifestation. An apparition or a shadow that is seen may have been caused by a projector being turned on and off remotely by the hoaxer or an accomplice. These RF detectors typically run $15 to $40 each.

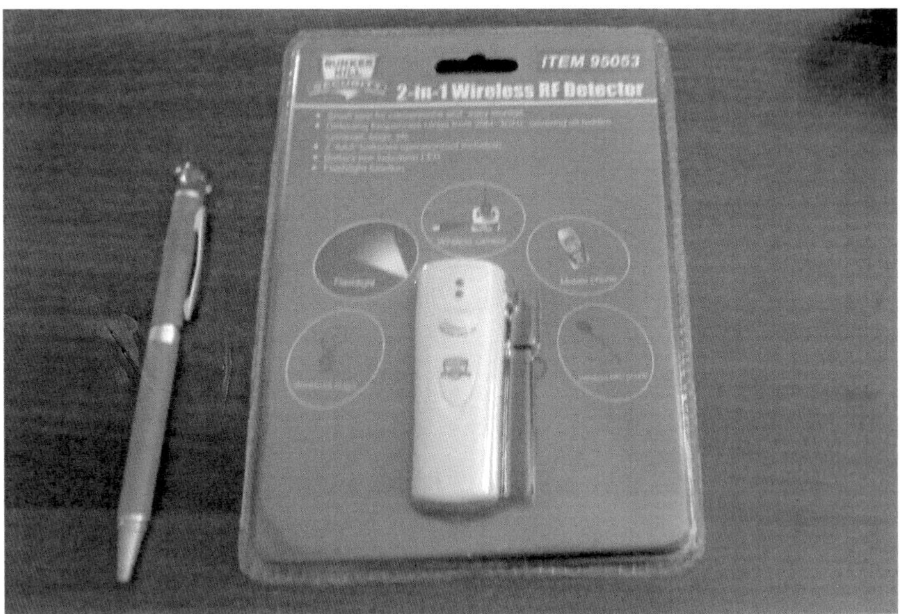

Radio frequency (RF) detection device.

Thermometers

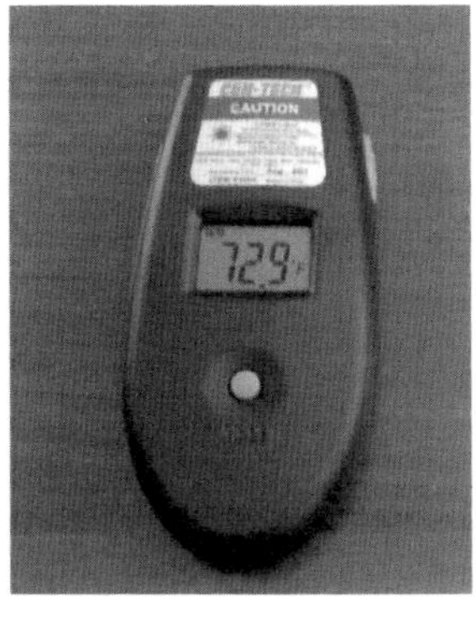

Non-contact temperature detector.

Thermometers are useful for detecting hot and cold spots in rooms and on surfaces that could be a manifestation of a paranormal entity. Non-contact thermometers (such as those on the Mel Meter) are useful in detecting temperature fluctuations of the air in a room. The contact thermometer uses a light beam to detect the temperature of a surface. The contact thermometer is useful to identify the possible causes of temperature changes in the air, such as detecting the change in the temperature reading of a vent duct in a ceiling or high up on a wall (which would be an indicator that an air conditioner or heater may have turned on causing the change in temperature observed). Estimated cost is $20 to $40.

Audio Recorders

Audio recorders are useful to pick up and record any noise or voice that may be able to be heard by a human ear. The recorder can be immediately played back by the investigator to hear the sound or voice again and to try to determine the nature of the sound and the cause. Audio recorders have also been used in lieu of pencils and notebooks during a lights-out investigation, as it is difficult for investigators to write when it is pitch black in a building. These recorders are also useful in detecting EVPs, though these are usually found after the investigation during the examination of the evidence. Estimated cost is $20 to $80.

Walkie-Talkies

Walkie-talkies are useful tools to keep investigators in contact with one another, especially if an emergency occurs. While the walkie-talkies themselves do not assist in detecting paranormal manifestations (do not expect ghosts to call you on a walkie-talkie), if an unusual noise or voice is detected by investigators, they can use the walkie-talkie to contact one another to rule out any possible investigator-generated sounds. Multi-channel walkie-talkies are relatively inexpensive, running from $25 to $75 each.

Electro Magnetic Field (EMF) Detector

The EMF detector is the heart and soul of the investigation effort. An entity trying to materialize uses energy. An entity trying to move an object uses energy. An entity trying to possess someone uses energy. An entity trying to create a noise or audibly communicate uses energy. This use or translation of energy by an entity is almost always manifested with either a burst or a continuous discharge of electromagnetism. This electromagnetism is a field that is detectable by the investigators' instruments at various distances depending on the electromagnetic field strength. The more energy being used or translated, the higher the electromagnetic field that is generated and detectable. The higher and stronger the electromagnetic field, the farther away it can be detected and the stronger it is up close. Electromagnetic energy is measured in units known as MilliGauss (mG).

Regretfully, paranormal entities are not the only things that are able to generate an electromagnetic field. Electromagnetic energy can also be generated by and be detected in the vicinity of all electrical equipment and appliances that are plugged into or hardwired into a building's electrical system. Lights, fans, extension cords, receptacles, switches, clocks, computers, televisions, refrigerators, even electrical wiring that is concealed in walls, floors and ceilings will give off an electromagnetic field that can be detectable. Even a common cellphone transmitting and receiving may be sensed and identified by the EMF detector as an electromagnetic field.

When an unusual EMF reading is detected, the investigator must look around and try to act as a paranormal debunker. They must attempt to determine a natural and scientific explanation for the unusual electromagnetic readings by checking around for any local energized electrical equipment that may be operating. Also, they will need to look for wires that may be present or in the walls, floors or ceiling or maybe even the silenced cellphone that is in one of the paranormal investigators' pockets.

These electromagnetic field detectors are typically available for between $50 to $300 depending on the specific type of detector that the investigator would prefer to use.

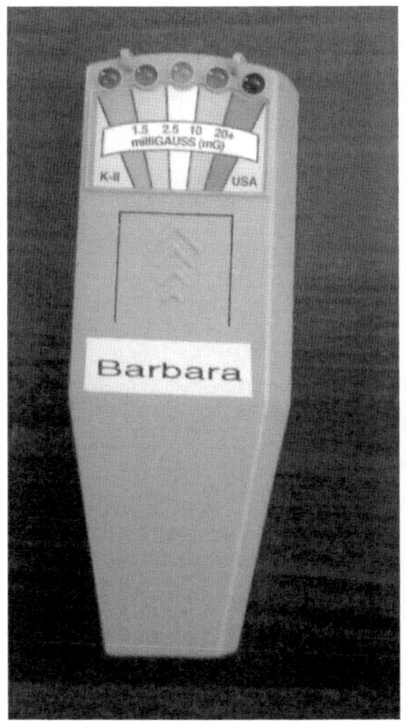

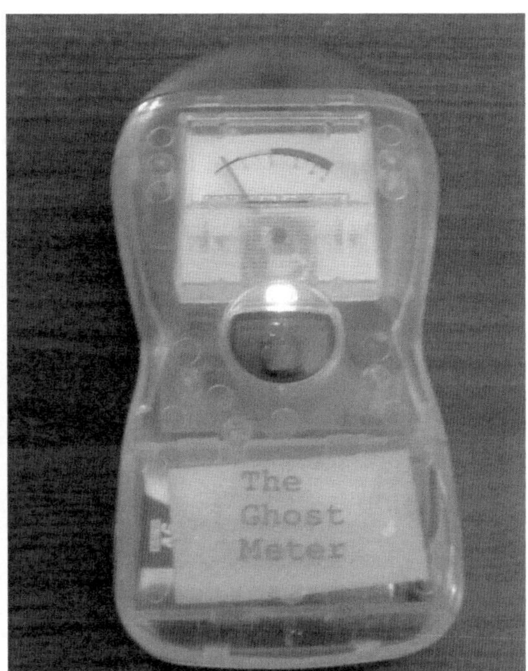

Above, left: K II meter can measure 0 to 20 mG by illuminating lights in sequence.

Above, right: The Ghost Meter can measure 0 to 5 mG with an analog dial and light display.

Right: The Mel Meter can measure both 0 to 20,000 mG and air temperature in a digital display.

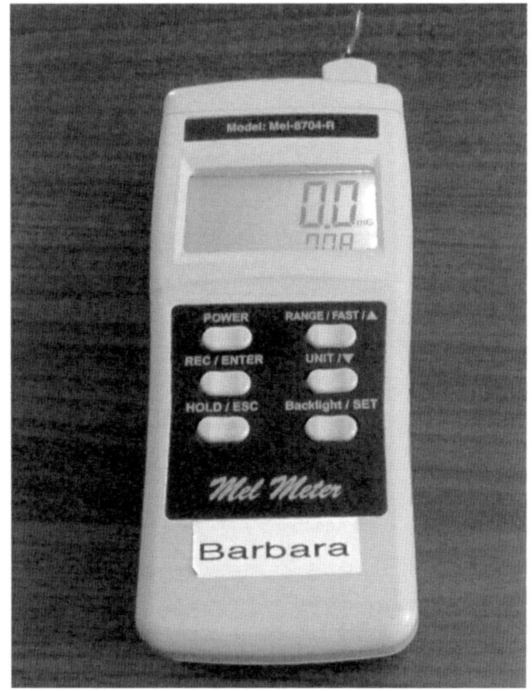

MOTION-ACTIVATED INFRARED CAMERAS

These cameras are popular with hunters who want to identify lucrative locations to pursue their avocation. When entities materialize, they generate motion. Some entities may be too shy and reserved or perhaps they just don't want to appear during the daytime. In any event, these cameras can be placed in an area that is the alleged haunt of an entity, and it can be left there. If a paranormal entity (or a small furry animal) moves or materializes in the camera's view and range, the camera will record still photos of it. (Some more expensive models will take video.) It will also use infrared lights to illuminate the area to allow a clear picture of the entity (or animal), even in a pitch-black closet. These cameras are available from $75 to $300.

DIGITAL CAMERA

The digital camera is one of the other essential tools required for paranormal investigations. The digital camera can provide essential evidence toward proving the reliability of the paranormal encounter reportedly experienced by the investigator. Experienced investigators have often found the need to keep spare batteries for the digital cameras on hand. Some entities are reported to have the ability to use the chemical energy potential of the batteries in the cameras and convert the chemical energy to ectoplasmic energy for use in manifestations. Most digital cameras that are available on the market are capable of both still photography and video and are able to provide a backup source of video recording in case of the failure of the primary recorders. Digital cameras are widely available for $60 to $200. Digital cameras are also readily available in pawnshops for significantly less money.

VIDEO CAMERA

The video camera is another vital element required to provide scientifically acceptable evidence in a paranormal investigation. While digital cameras can provide quite a bit of information (a picture is worth a thousand words), showing a door or window moving without human intervention is much more impressive and would provide a higher degree of acceptable proof of an entity's physical manifestations. The video cameras can also act as a backup to the investigation's audio recording devices, as the vast majority record audio as well as video. Video cameras are widely available in stores for between $100 and $500. Video cameras are also widely available in pawnshops for a significant savings.

INFRARED AND FULL SPECTRUM STILL CAMERA

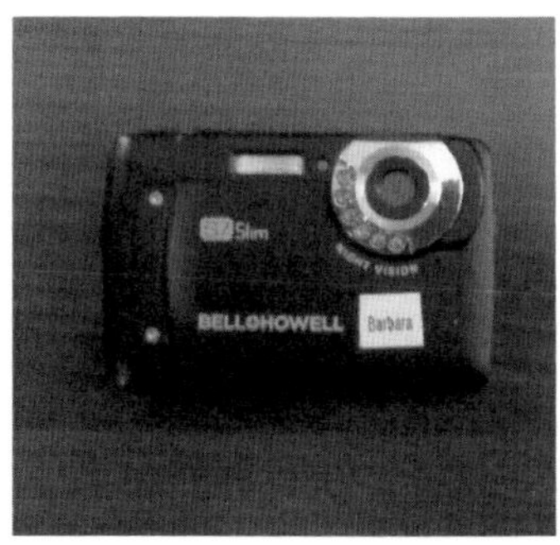

Digital infrared camera manufactured by Bell and Howell with an infrared flash.

There are some entities that may only be visible in the infrared or ultraviolet spectrum, which are light spectrums that are typically not visible to the human eye. Infrared still cameras can provide a scientifically acceptable level of evidence of paranormal entities that are operating at reduced ectoplasmic energy levels in the infrared frequency of light. Full spectrum cameras are able to detect entities that manifest in either infrared or ultraviolet. Neither the infrared nor the full spectrum digital still cameras are commonly available in electronic retail stores, and they tend to be a little more expensive than the regularly available digital still cameras. These infrared cameras are available from $100 to $2,600 and are not typically available from pawnshops.

INFRARED VIDEO CAMERA

Infrared video cameras are not as common as regular video cameras. Infrared cameras allow video recording of paranormal entities that are visible to the human eye and those that operate on lower frequencies of light and use less ectoplasmic energy to manifest. Unfortunately, some companies have been concerned about being sued because of the reported infrared viewing ability of the video cameras. Under certain limited conditions, it may be possible for these cameras to take photographs and video through people's clothing. Investigators must be aware of this possible adverse ability and take measures to protect themselves, other investigators and their virtue. These infrared video cameras are typically available for between $150 to $1,000 and have quite often been found for significantly reduced amounts at pawnshops.

Infrared video cameras will use infrared lights on front of the camera for video recording in low light conditions. These cameras will typically have a night vision activating switch on the side or the top to activate the infrared lights.

DOWSING RODS

Dowsing rods are listed close to last because of their limited use in scientifically reliable paranormal investigations. While there are those who swear by their use and testify to their accuracy, quite a few people believe dowsing rods give the investigator false readings of the paranormal due to the concept of the self-fulfilling prophesy. The idea behind the self-fulfilling prophesy is that if the individual believes something strongly enough, it will occur. In the case of paranormal research and investigations, it is a concern that dowsing rods will present the answers the investigator wants to find, not because of paranormal influence, but because of the user's subconscious desire for it to be true.

Dowsing rods have been used to locate underground water and to locate lost personal items.

Albert Einstein is reported to have stated: "I know very well that many scientists consider dowsing as a type of ancient superstition. According to my conviction this is, unjustified. The dowsing rod is a simple instrument which shows the uncanny reaction of the human nervous system to certain factors which are unknown to us at this time."[12]

Dowsing rods were used in the Middle Ages to divine the truth in people's testimonies similar to what a lie detector endeavors to do today. They probably had the same mixed results, as current lie detectors respond to the nervous system of the individual holding it more than the research subject.

Dowsing rods may well demonstrate some nervous system activity of the investigator to an external paranormal presence, but as they are unreliable, their use in scientifically based paranormal research and investigations should be minimized.

Dowsing rods can be manufactured by the investigator out of wood, or they are available in copper at reasonable cost, between $15 and $50.

Ghost Box

A ghost box, or spirit box as it is sometimes called, is a tool that is used by paranormal researchers to attempt to verbally communicate with paranormal entities. It is a paranormal theory that paranormal entities are able to project their voices on a variety of changing frequencies that are not typically audible to the human ear. The ghost box is a radio that has been modified to continuously scan frequencies with the stopping function disabled. The sounds generated tend to be white noise, static and possibly snatches of radio transmissions. The radio transmissions are further reduced by encasing the radio in a double aluminum shell to restrict the amount of radio transmissions that are able to reach the receiver and be broadcast on the speaker. The result is the only noise that should be audible on the speaker would be white noise, static and ethereal communications.

Pendulums

Pendulums have been used in the same situations as dowsing rods and suffer from the same drawbacks. The pendulum would be held by an individual and move in a certain direction. Asking questions could result in the movement representing yes or no, and if the individual was searching for an object, it would supposedly pull toward the lost object. The use of pendulums in a scientific investigation should be prohibited.

Pendulums are reasonably priced, typically between $10 and $50.

GLOSSARY

ANGEL. Angels are considered by religious individuals to be positive energy entities that are in the service of and doing the bidding of God. These paranormal entities are typically believed in by a wide variety of religious practitioners, and in most cases, they are considered to represent the theological concept of good. Angels are considered by most occupants and investigators to be nonthreatening and represent no cause for concern

APPARITION. An apparition is the unexplained sudden physical appearance of what seems to be a deceased person or animal or a portion thereof. These apparitions are typically dark, translucent and could materialize as a shadow, a full-body apparition or, more commonly, as a smaller portion of a human or animal body. An apparition has usually been found to be a nonthreatening entity but may be disconcerting to the observer.

CLAIRAUDIENCE. The ability to hear things such as voices not typically audible within normal hearing ranges.

COLD SPOT. A small, readily defined area of temperature that is lower than the ambient temperature by at least ten degrees that is not explained by other natural or mechanical causes such as vents, drafts, air conditioning, uninsulated exterior walls and so forth. It is believed cold spots originate from entities' use of thermal energy to allow them to manifest themselves.

DEBUNK. Debunking is the act of an individual investigator to provide a rational and reasonable scientific explanation for the detected evidence of a paranormal entity's manifestations.

DEMON. Demons have been found by researchers to be extremely malevolent spirits that are almost always actively aggressive and antagonistic toward occupants and investigators. If there has been major damage done to personal property or to the building, violent physical attacks against occupants or investigators or the violent possession of a human occupant or investigator, it would probably be indicative of the presence of a demon. Demons are entities that are better left to the careful ministrations of exorcists from a religious organization or to a professional demonologist and should be avoided by occupants, researchers and investigators if at all possible.

DEMONOLOGIST. An individual who specializes in the study and exorcism of demons and other evil entities.

DEVIL. Devils are considered by religious individuals to be extremely negative energy entities. The term *devil* is sometimes used in literature interchangeably with *demon*. These extremely malevolent spirits are typically believed in by a variety of religious individuals and are usually considered to represent the theological concept of evil. Most religious leaders have preached that devils were originally angels fallen from the grace of God. Devils are entities that are better left to the careful ministrations of exorcists from a religious organization or to a professional demonologist and should be avoided by occupants, researchers and investigators if at all possible.

DJINN. A djinn appears to be an Islamic version of an imp but just a little more dangerous. Djinn would almost seem to be equivalent to a lesser form of a demon. Djinn are reported to act in ways similar to imps such as taking objects, moving items around, starting fires and generally harassing people. They also are reported to be able to take possession of people just like demons do. While these entities appear to be less dangerous than demons, they would still require the use of religious exorcists or a professional demonologist to exorcise them and should be avoided by occupants, researchers and investigators if at all possible.

DOWSING. Dowsing is the act of using a Y-shaped rod or a pair of rods held in the hands to locate water or minerals, to locate missing objects or to communicate with entities. Dowsing rods were also used in the Middle Ages as an early form of a lie detector.

ECTOPLASM. Ectoplasm is believed to be the material substance that entities are made up of. Residual ectoplasm is not usually found in large quantities and can be observed as a mist or as a trace substance that is sometimes left behind on materials by certain types of manifestations. Residual ectoplasm will either rapidly evaporate or be quickly absorbed by materials it was deposited on upon the departure of an observed entity. Ectoplasm may occasionally erroneously be referred to by investigators as mist, although mist may well be made up of ectoplasm.

ELECTROMAGNETIC FIELD (EMF). An EMF field is usually found in the vicinity of electrical and electronic devices. Mild EMF fields are also found around living beings and have been referred to by some as a living being's aura. An entity trying to materialize or cause a change in the material world uses ectoplasmic energy. This use or translation of energy by an entity is almost always manifested with either a burst or a continuous discharge of electromagnetism. This electromagnetism is a field that is detectable by the investigators' instruments at various distances depending on the electromagnetic field strength.

ELECTRONIC VOICE PHENOMENA (EVP). EVPs are the unexplainable voices or sounds that are heard by investigators only when electronic recordings made during an investigation are played back. The entities that are responsible for these audible manifestations are typically nonthreatening and are usually not associated with any other physical manifestation that may be a cause for concern to occupants. Care must be taken by the audio specialist to ensure that these audio anomalies are not the noises or soft voices of other investigators or occupants farther away from the recorder.

ELEMENTAL. An elemental is a paranormal entity that is believed to be just another name for a demon. While there may be a wide variety of elementals having a wide variety of different reported abilities, the same can be said of demons. They are reportedly entities of negative ectoplasmic energy that have a very hostile attitude toward humans and our plane of existence.

EMPATH. Individuals who appear to be more sensitive than others to a paranormal entity.

ENTITY. Entity is a very generic name for all forms of paranormal creatures, but it is more typically used by paranormal researchers to refer to formerly living persons or animals.

FEAR CAGE. A small, well defined, enclosed area (such as a closet or small room) with unusually high EMF readings. Typically this is an area that will generate negative feelings (uneasiness, paranoia or fear) in the investigator or occupants.

FULL-BODY APPARITION. A full-bodied apparition is the unexplained appearance of the entire body of an animal or person.

GHOST. A ghost is the spirit of a dead person or animal believed to be associated with a specific location or object. Ghosts may present as physical apparitions, nonthreatening movement of objects or simply as audible effects such as taps, creaking noises, footsteps or EVPs.

GHOST BOX or SPIRIT BOX. A ghost box, or spirit box as it is sometimes called, is a tool used by paranormal researchers to attempt to verbally communicate with paranormal entities.

HOT SPOT. A small, readily defined area of temperature that is higher than the ambient temperature by at least ten degrees that is not explained by other natural or mechanical causes such as vents, drafts, heaters, uninsulated exterior walls and so forth. This is much less common than a cold spot and is typically to be found in the vicinity of demons and devils.

IMP. An imp is a malevolent entity that purposefully acts to harass occupants as well as investigators. Imps have a tendency to play tricks, pull pranks and repeatedly harass the occupants and paranormal investigators. They are able to cause a variety of minor damage to property, rearrange or move objects, create a variety of odors and occasionally to start small fires. If an olfactory manifestation is present, the entity is probably an imp. While these entities are much less dangerous than demons, they still require the use of exorcists from a religious organization or a professional demonologist to exorcise them and they should be avoided by occupants, researchers and investigators if at all possible.

IMPRINT. Significant events or strong-willed individuals can occasionally leave a copy or record of themselves on places or things. These manifestations may repeat over and over again without changing.

INFRARED (IR). Infrared light is a low frequency light that is not visible to humans without the use of special devices.

INTELLIGENT HAUNTING. An intelligent haunting is a haunting in which the observed entity appears to be capable of free thought and can interact with the investigators or occupants.

KINETIC ENERGY. Kinetic energy is that energy required to accelerate an object of a specific mass from a state of rest to a specific velocity. Kinetic energy is also energy possessed by objects in motion.

LIGHTS-OUT INVESTIGATION. A paranormal investigation with all possible light sources extinguished, typically conducted indoors and at night.

LOST TIME. A difference in time passage that is temporally inexplicable.

MANIFESTATION. A physically observable phenomenon typically associated with paranormal activity. If a researcher or occupant is able to see it, hear it, touch it, smell it, taste it or is capture it on electronic, audio or camera equipment, it is a manifestation.

MIST. Mist is an observable yet inexplicable phenomenon resembling a small cloud or haze that is believed to be made up of some sort of ectoplasm. When a mist is observed, it will quite often be accompanied by a localized cold spot. The mist is usually found to be several feet above the ground, and it may be found stationary or, less frequently, moving around. As mist may perhaps be made up of ectoplasm, investigators will occasionally erroneously refer to mist as ectoplasm and tend to use the terms interchangeably.

ORB. An orb is a globe-shaped concentration of energy appearing as white spots in photographs or video taken of reported haunted locations.

PARANORMAL. Paranormal means "beyond the normal" and refers to something that science is unable to explain at this time. An interchangeable word for paranormal would be supernatural.

PARTIAL-BODY APPARITION. A partial-bodied apparition is the unexpected sudden appearance before an investigator or occupant of a portion of the body of a deceased person or animal.

PERIPHERAL DRIFT ILLUSION. Peripheral drift illusion is the illusion of motion of an object seen in peripheral vision. It is believed to be caused by the difference in the detection methods utilized by the different components of the eye. The eye tends to continuously scan, and the rods are the primary receptor in peripheral vision. Rods are more sensitive to motion, and stationary objects may be undetectable until there is a movement of the head or of the eyes. This is a relative motion between the observer and the object and not an actual motion of the perceived object. This results in an optical illusion of motion.

POLTERGEIST. German expression that means "noisy ghost." This type of paranormal entity is typically identified as possessing only an audible presence or manifestation, and they have been found by researchers to be very nonthreatening, although the noises that are heard may be very disconcerting to those hearing them.

RADIO FREQUENCY. Radio frequency is the range of wavelengths that an electronic signal such as television or radio would typically be transmitted or received on. This frequency wavelength ranges anywhere from 3 kilohertz up to 300 gigahertz. This is the frequency range that small audio and video transmitters and receivers (spy cams) operate on.

RADIO FREQUENCY DETECTOR. Radio frequency signal detectors are a tool utilized by paranormal investigators to help ensure a more scientifically accurate paranormal investigation is conducted. These RF detectors are not primarily used to detect paranormal entities but instead are used to weed out potential hoaxes. When a radio frequency signal is detected by an investigator, it means someone is broadcasting or receiving something (it could be just somebody's cell phone they forgot to turn off prior to the investigation).

RESIDUAL HAUNTING. A residual haunting is a frequently recurring, nonthreatening, visible and/or audible manifestation that does not appear to have any purposeful action or thought. This is similar to watching or listening to a videotape or audiotape over and over. Residual haunting has also been known to be called after-echoes by some. Examples would be footsteps heard over and over on a stairway or in a hall, doorknobs that rattle periodically or apparitions seen performing the same actions again and again. An inanimate version of a residual haunting would be the ghostly appearance of the Flying Dutchman seen by sailors.

SHADOW. Shadows tend to present as dark apparitions that are usually very difficult to discern by eye. Typically, shadows are seen as translucent and are better observed on video or in photographs. Investigators may best be able to find shadows as motion seen out of the corners of their eyes. While shadows are not typically associated with other negative manifestations, and would tend to be able to utilize less ectoplasmic energy, they may be quite disconcerting to those observing them.

SHADOW PERSON. A shadow person is another name that is occasionally used to refer to a spirit.

SPIRIT. A spirit is believed to be an entity that probably was not born an earthly creature such as a human or an animal. An example of an entity considered a spirit would be an angel, a demon, a devil, a djinn and so on. These entities have also been referred to as shadow persons in a variety of literature. Spirits require the use of exorcists from a religious organization or a professional demonologist to exorcise them, and they should be avoided by occupants, researchers and investigators if at all possible.

STREAK. A streak is an unexplained line of light that is captured on photographs—similar to an orb but lengthened. A true streak would be made of ectoplasm and would be accompanied by high EMF readings. Investigators almost never report the presence of a streak during an investigation; they are only found during the review of the evidence collected during it. For this reason, they are typically explained away as camera movement during the taking of the photograph.

SUPERNATURAL. Activities or manifestations that are caused by conscious will of some paranormal entity.

TOUCHED. The physical contact that may occasionally occur between an entity being observed and a paranormal investigator or occupant.

ULTRAVIOLET (UV). Ultraviolet light is a long wavelength light that is not visible to humans without the use of special devices.

VIBRATIONAL ENERGY. Vibrational energy is believed to be the basic energy that forms all physical matter. Some forms of vibrational energy may be visible to humans (physical matter), and some may only be able to be detected by a variety of sensitive electronic instruments (sound waves, light waves, microwaves, electromagnetic waves and so on).

VORTEX. A vortex is defined as a small area of highly concentrated electromagnetic energy that may be captured in photographs that are taken during a paranormal investigation. A vortex has typically been found in the shape of a V or a rod and is normally associated with cold spots. There are theories that these may be the spirits of former residents or may be the physical manifestation of spirits traveling between dimensions.

WHITE NOISE. White noise is random sound waves that are generated by specific electronic devices that cover a wide range of frequencies. This is sometimes referred to as static.

NOTES

1. Texas State Historic Society, Bell County, https://tshaonline.org/handbook/online/articles/hcb06.
2. The City of Killeen charter has been updated, removing all reference to the watchmen, as they are no longer authorized. It was contained in the old city charter (section 17) that was replaced in 2010. I have a copy of the old charter provided to me by the city secretary, https://library.municode.com/tx/killeen/codes/code_of_ordinances.
3. *Los Angeles Herald-Examiner*, February 23, 1965; *Leavenworth (KS) Times*, February 24, 1965; *Brownwood (TX) Bulletin*, February 23, 1965; *The Eagle* (Bryan, TX), February 23, 1965.
4. The Bloody Bell County years vary depending on which old-timer you ask. Generally speaking, they started in the late 1860s and ran through about 1930. A good reference for the period is a book by Rick Miller, *Bloody Bell County: Vignettes of Violence and Mayhem in Central Texas* (Belton, TX: Bell County Museum, 2011).
5. A question of law is decided by a judge. A question of fact is decided by either a jury (in a jury trial) or the judge (in a bench trial without a jury). By making this a question of law, the judge decided there was no question of fact regarding the haunting. There was no question of fact, by law the house was haunted.
6. *Stambovsky v. Ackley*, 169 A.D.2d 254, 572 N.Y.S.2d 672, 1991 NY App. Div.; John Patrick Schutz, "Nyack's 'Legally' Haunted House," At Home in Nyack, October 29, 2010, https://athomeinnyack.wordpress.com/2010/10/29/nyacks-legally-haunted-house.

7. Clara Moskowitz, "Fact or Fiction? Energy Can Neither Be Created Nor Destroyed," *Scientific American*, August 5, 2014, https://www.scientificamerican.com/article/energy-can-neither-be-created-nor-destroyed.
8. Victor Zammit, "The Seven Laws of Psychic Energy," May 2001, http://www.victorzammit.com/articles/sevenlaws.html.
9. "Flash Reflections from Floating Dust Particles," https://web.archive.org/web/20050727000507/http://home.fujifilm.com/products/digital/shooting/flash.html.
10. C.A. Johnson, "Motion Sensitivity in Central and Peripheral Vision," *American Journal of Optometry and Physiological Optics* 63, no. 2 (February 1986): 104–7.
11. J. Faubert and A.M. Herbert, "The Peripheral Drift Illusion: A Motion Illusion in the Visual Periphery," *Perception* 28, no. 5 (1999): 617–21.
12. "Einstein Thought Dowsing Was Genuine and Now 17 Experts Will Explain Why," Webwire, September 14, 2012, https://www.sott.net/article/251269-Einstein-Thought-Dowsing-Was-Genuine-and-Now-17-Experts-Will-Explain-Why.

About the Author

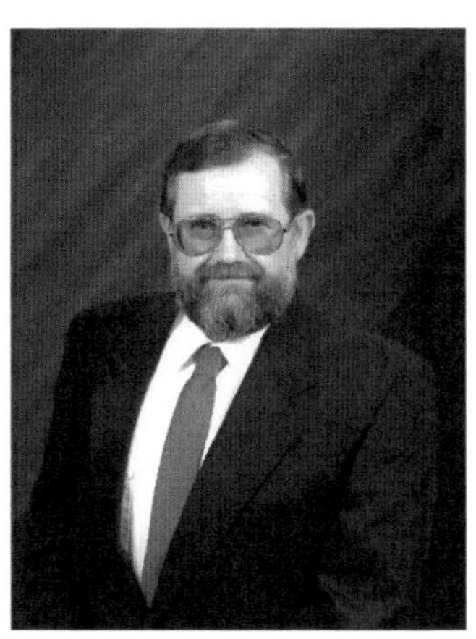

Chet Southworth spent five years laboring in a steel foundry, twenty years in nuclear engineering, five years in corporate management and nine years in city management. He has a bachelor of science degree from the University of New York, a master's in human resources development and organizational development from Friends University, a master's in business administration from Texas A&M–Central Texas and a doctor of jurisprudence from Texas Tech University. Chet has been a paranormal researcher, investigator and primarily a debunker for over thirty years. He currently resides in Killeen, Texas, with his wife, Barbara, several cats and Pooka, the spirit of Barbara's deceased pet.